Make Your Own Christmas Tree Decorations

Festive and Fun Craft Projects to Decorate Your Christmas Tree

by Susan Yeates

www.magenta-sky.com

Bright Pen

Visit us online at www.authorsonline.co.uk

This book is dedicated to my sewing bees

Acknowledgements

I would firstly like to thank all my lovely friends and family (crafty and non-crafty) for your help and encouragement with writing this book. I am also hugely grateful to everyone who has contributed to the book, especially Angela and Roxy, the two lovely creatives that helped to bring this 'vision' of a Christmas craft book to life. I would also like to thank my collection of enthusiastic proof-readers and Edison for all his love and support throughout. You are all amazing!

For more art, craft and printmaking
books and resources
by Susan Yeates
please visit:

www.magenta-sky.com

Follow us on Twitter:
@MagentaSky1

2

A Bright Pen Book
Copyright © Susan Yeates 2014

Cover photos: Angela Melling, Picturia Commercial Photography
Lead graphic designer and cover design: Roxy Da Silva
Finished product photography: Angela Melling, Picturia Commercial Photography 2014
Additional photos: Tracey Haskins: Bermuda Door Wreath, 2010 (p.6–7), Tree/Drummers, 2013
(p.7) and Jessica Hocking: Bella, 2013 (p.103)
All 'making' photography and additional graphic design: Susan Yeates

British Library Cataloguing in Publication Data.
A catalogue record for this book is available from the
British Library.

ISBN: 978-0-7552-1651-2

Authors OnLine Ltd
19 The Cinques
Gamlingay, Sandy
Bedfordshire SG19 3NU
England

This book is also available in e-book format, details of which are available at
www.authorsonline.co.uk

CONTENTS

Welcome to this crafty book all about how to create your own unique Christmas tree decorations! Choose a project and get stuck in...

Susan

Introduction   p.6–9

Section 1
Baubles, Beads & Sparkles

1.	Christmas beads	p.12–13
2.	Crystal stars	p.14–15
3.	Rhinestone baubles	p.16–17
4.	Pompom snowballs	p.18–20
5.	Baubles with ribbon	p.22–23

Section 2
Sewing Projects

6.	Patchwork stars	p.26–27
7.	Fabric hearts	p.28–29
8.	Gingerbread man	p.30–32
9.	Christmas pudding	p.34–35
10.	Christmas stocking	p.36–37
11.	Mini Christmas bunting	p.38–40
12.	Tartan trees	p.42–43
13.	Christmas robin	p.44–46

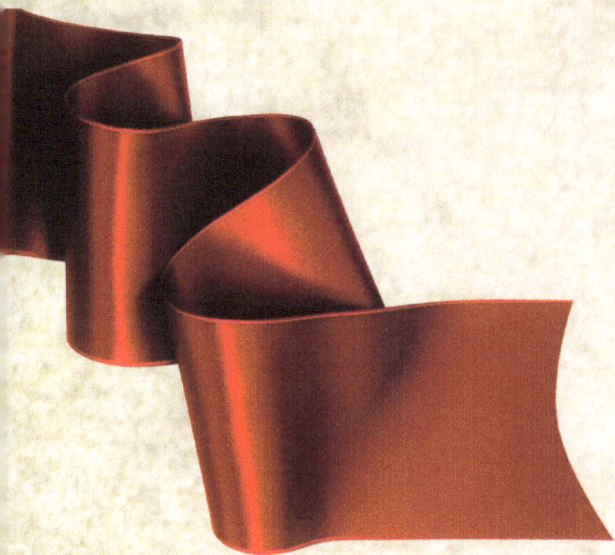

Section 3
From the Kitchen

14.	Traditional pomanders	p.50–51
15.	Carved fruit decorations	p.52–53
16.	Dried fruit decorations	p.54–56
17.	Salt dough shapes	p.58–60
18.	Salt dough photo frames	p.62–64
19.	Walnut wonders	p.66–67
20.	Cinnamon bundles	p.68–69

Section 4
Let's get Creative!

21.	Crochet baubles	p.72–73
22.	Modelling clay puddings	p.74–75
23.	Modelling clay holly leaves	p.76
24.	Modelling clay candy canes	p.77–78
25.	Crochet snowflake	p.80–81
26.	Crochet snowman	p.82–84

Section 5
Thrifty Treats

27.	Mini presents	p.88–89
28.	Christmas gold cones	p.90–91
29.	Fabric bundles	p.92–93
30.	Buttontastic wreaths	p.94–95
31.	Origami stars	p.96–98

| **Templates** | p.100–101 |
| **How-To Guides** | p.102–103 |

INTRODUCTION

The spectacle of putting up the tree...

Christmas memories...

One of my earliest Christmas memories involves my sister and I as young children helping our parents to place shiny baubles on a sweet smelling, freshly cut Christmas tree. We would then sit cross-legged in front of the tree as the living room lights would be switched off and the Christmas tree lights switched on to an excited chorus of '*oooos*' and '*aaaaahs*' – **Christmas had begun!**

This memory has stuck with me throughout the years and even now, the excitement and magic of Christmas only truly starts when a tree is selected, a space is cleared for it to reside and it gets covered in a multitude of decorations ready for presents to be laid at its base.

In public spaces, the ceremonial 'switching on of the Christmas tree lights' has become a part of the yearly ritual throughout late November and early December, often marking the opening of late night shopping and the start of local festivities. National celebrities are regularly invited to carry out the actual switching on of the lights and countless families bring their children along to watch in awe as lights come on, as music plays and as mulled wine gets sipped by chilled bodies (not by the children I may add!).

Essentially, putting up the Christmas tree is an event to be savoured and enjoyed. Whether this is in the comfort of your own home or out in public, it is always warming and fun; and for me marks one of my favourite times of year – **CHRISTMAS!**

The creative and crafty tree...

Whether you choose to put your tree up as soon as the weather gets cold, on the first weekend in December or you wait until the excitement of Christmas Eve, a beautifully decorated Christmas tree is, in my humble opinion, the focal point of the home over the festive season.

For years now I have made my own hand-made decorations to place on the Christmas tree. A new one (or two) each year is carefully crafted to add to the growing collection of hand-made ornaments. This makes my tree unique, different every year and just a little bit special, as I remember the time I made each item and decide where on the tree to hang each piece. It also gives me the chance to learn and practise a new craft and create a number of little gifts to give out to family or friends.

So from this collection of hand-crafted decorations I have picked my favourites to include here and of course some brand new designs created especially for the book. My aim is to share with you some of the festive and creative fun I have had over the years, and to encourage everyone to learn some new crafts in the process.

The projects in this book...

Each decoration in this book is a separate craft project in its own right. Therefore this book gives each reader a chance to try out a variety of different crafts through these festive mini-projects. All projects can be created in the comfort of your own home and all with a small selection of materials available from local art shops, craft stores or the supermarket.

Most of the projects take under an hour to complete and vary from crochet to sewing to gluing and even a spot of origami!

Section 1 | Baubles, Beads and Sparkles This book begins with some simple beads and baubles projects. Sometimes sparkly and shiny, sometimes colourful and simple, this collection of 5 projects is a great place to get started.

Section 2 | Sewing Projects It's time to get out the sewing kit! We work through 7 separate sewing projects from a cute felt gingerbread man to mini-bunting for the tree. These projects use a variety of sewing techniques and includes both hand-sewing and machine-sewing.

Section 3 | From the Kitchen This section takes us into the kitchen to create a selection of ornaments either made from food-based ingredients or that require cooking. Salt dough shapes, cinnamon sticks and traditional pomanders to mention a few…

Section 4 | Let's Get Creative Does what it says – gets just a little bit more creative! We explore 3 exciting crochet projects and get modelling with some 'Fimo' modelling clay.

Section 5 | Thrifty Treats And to finish, these projects show you how to use up all your Christmas scraps, such as wrapping paper, last year's Christmas cards or even found items for some almost free hand-made ornaments.

So here we are – over 30 separate creative projects to decorate your tree. Enjoy getting festive and crafty this year!

Merry Christmas!

Susan

History of Christmas Trees...

So, throughout this book we are making special crafty projects for your Christmas tree... Let's explore a little bit about the history and background of the Christmas tree. It is a regular fixture of the festive season but where did this tradition come from and why do we feel the need to cut down a living tree, decorate it with ornaments and/or lights and place it in our homes?

Christmas trees are usually of the evergreen conifer variety such as spruce, fir or pine. Chosen to fit into a room or larger for external trees, we either pot them or place them in simple stands. In recent years, to avoid the plethora of needles falling from a live tree and the care needed to water it, many people instead select from a variety of artificial trees that can be reused year after year.

Traditionally Christmas trees in the 18th century were decorated with edible and natural items such as apples, nuts, gingerbread or other food. Candles were a regular feature as well until the invention of electric Christmas lights as a safer option. In today's society there are so many possible decorations to choose from including baubles, sweets, ribbon, tinsel, garlands, chocolate coins, candy canes and more traditional elements such as stars or angels to represent elements of the Nativity.

Evergreen trees have traditionally been thought to keep away witches, ghosts, evil spirits, and illness and many different cultures have used the boughs and branches of these trees to do just this. Sometimes known as a 'Yule' tree, the Christmas tree is an extension and development of these ancient and folklore traditions, modified for a modern society celebrating an important festival in the Christian calendar. Christmas also falls on the Winter Solstice and its traditions and heritage also borrow from these pagan roots.

It is a widely held belief that the modern Christmas tree tradition stemmed from early modern Germany. This itself had roots in the 16th and possibly 15th centuries where devout Christians brought decorated trees into their homes. However, the first documented use of a tree at Christmas and New Year celebrations is in the town square of Riga, the capital of Latvia, in the year 1510. It is also believed that Martin Luther, the 16th-century Protestant reformer, first brought the Christmas tree into the home and added lighted candles to it. Walking toward his home one winter evening, he was amazed by the brilliant stars twinkling amidst the trees. To recapture the scene for his family, he put up a tree in the main room and placed candles on its branches.

However, it is from the second half of the 19th century that its popularity in the UK spread widely as a family tradition. In particular, the young Queen Victoria was captivated by a Christmas tree being placed in her room every Christmas as a child. Then after her marriage to Prince Albert in 1841 and a Christmas tree was put up at Windsor Castle in 1848, the custom was even more widespread throughout the UK and US, with aspiring middle-class families following the trend set by the royal family. The tradition was also gaining mentions in newspapers, paintings and even books on the topic and by the 1920's was common through all social classes and in most public places.

Christmas trees are now grown commercially in Britain due to the high demand over the Christmas season and in 2013 approximately 8 million trees were grown in Britain alone for use in homes, shops and public spaces.

The Christmas tree is just one of many ancient Christmas traditions and in this book we are joining in by making some modern, hand-crafted decorations to place on its branches.

Section 1

BAUBLES, BEADS & SPARKLES

Baubles and ribbon,

Sparkles and beads,

These festive creations

Do more than just please...

CHRISTMAS BEADS

A great way to use up leftover colourful beads or an excuse to go shopping for more!

Tools and Materials:

- Gold or silver jewellery wire
- Jewellery pliers/cutters
- A piece of felt
- A selection of glass and/or plastic beads of different sizes

Instructions

1. Place a piece of felt onto your table and tip out your selection of beads onto it. The felt stops the beads from rolling around too much whilst you are working.

2. Arrange a selection of beads on the table in the order that you wish to arrange them. See photo 1.

3. Select some gold/silver wire that is thin enough to fit through the holes in your beads but strong enough to hold them. From this wire, cut off a piece that is the length that you wish your beaded decoration to be. Make sure to leave enough spare wire at the top to create a loop for hanging up the decoration when you are finished.

4. Place your first bead on one end of the wire about 1–2cm along. Fold the wire back on itself, over the bead and twist the end around to secure that first bead.

5. Begin to load on the rest of your beads from the other end of the wire, i.e. you are working from the bottom of the decoration upwards.

6. Once all your beads are loaded on, create a generous loop with the spare wire at the top and twist the end secure. Cut off any excess wire with some pliers and you are ready to hang it on the tree!

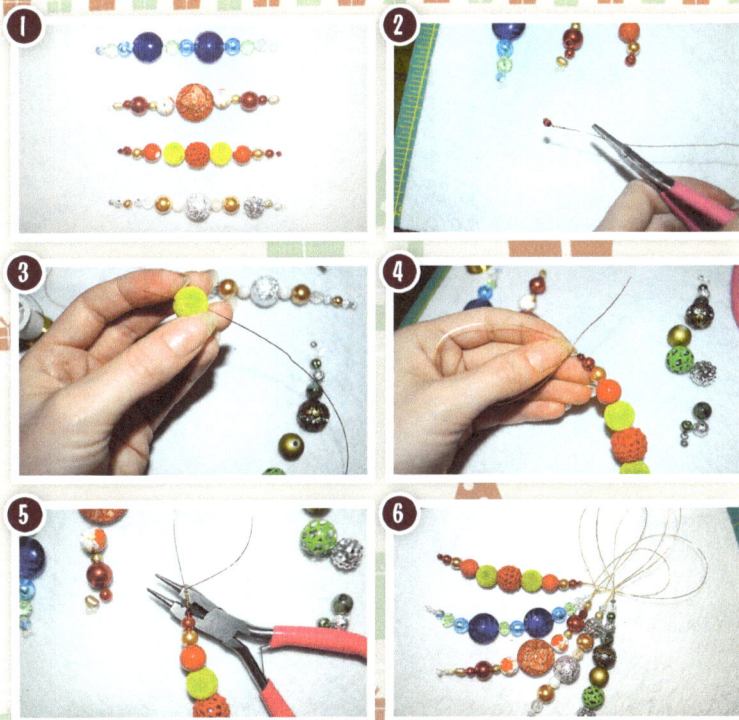

Tip:

If you don't have any wire available, this will also work using gold or silver thread instead. Just tie a knot at the bottom, load your beads (using a needle to help) and then tie a loop at the top.

CRYSTAL STARS

Twinkle twinkle little star...

Tools and Materials:

- Selection of coloured crystals
- Gold or silver jewellery wire
- Jewellery pliers/cutters
- Round nosed jewellery pliers
- Piece of thread

> *As a wanna-be jewellery maker, I have a stock of beautiful Swarovski crystals all neatly packed away in little plastic boxes, arranged by colour and size, perfect for this project. The crystals are beautiful and catch the light from your Christmas tree lights. Creating these stars is almost like creating twinkling jewellery to decorate your tree....*
>
> *Susan*

Instructions

1. Cut 3 lengths of jewellery wire approx 15–20cm each (or as large/small as you want your star to be).

2. Join these three strands of wire into a 6-pointed star shape by twisting them together in the middle over each other. This can be quite fiddly, so begin by connecting 2 wire strands and then add on the third.

3. Once the foundations of the star are created from your wire, select some crystals to use. In the example here I have used some small 3mm red diamond shape crystals alternating with some larger 6mm pale cream crystals.

4. Load the crystals onto one point of the star until you have just 5–10mm of wire remaining.

5. Using the rounded point of your jewellery pliers create a 3mm loop at the end of the wire to hold the crystals in place. Snip off any excess wire.

6. Thread the same combination of crystals (or a slightly different combination) onto the next wire point, and again create a 3mm loop of wire at the end to fix them in place.

7. Repeat with the remaining points of wire until your star is completely covered with crystals.

8. Thread a 15cm length of cotton onto one of the wire loops, tie a knot and use this to hang the star up.

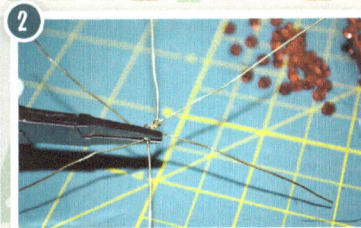

Tip:

Before you begin your star, lay out all the crystals you plan to use on your mat or table first. You can then choose the design you prefer and also work out exactly how long the wire points of the star need to be.

RHINESTONE BAUBLES

Your own glamorous glitter balls to add some special sparkle to any festive tree!

Tools and Materials:

- Foam balls
- Glue (e.g. Gem-Tac)
- Selection of rhinestone crystals (ideally SS16–SS20 size)
- 2 pins
- Piece of ribbon
- Piece of Blu-Tac
- Hairpin, pencil or similar

'Before you begin making the bauble, select some rhinestone crystals that you wish to use for the design. They come in various colours and sizes and can be bought online in small or large packs. I recommend using stones approx. SS16 – SS20 for these decorations but smaller and larger ones will also work. Make sure to purchase enough to cover your bauble and remember that the smaller the stone, the longer it will take you to stick them all on!' *Susan*

Instructions

1. Place a small ball of Blu-Tac on to the end of a hairpin or similar item (e.g. a pencil). This is what you will use to pick up the rhinestones as you go along.

2. Using some specialist glue (such as Gem-Tac) spread the glue onto the top of the bauble where you will start working.

3. Using your Blu-Tac'ed hairpin, pick up a rhinestone and stick it in place on the top of the bauble into the glue. Work slowly and carefully, gradually sticking on the crystals one by one next to each other. The closer the crystals are to each other, the more effective the decoration will be and the less the foam ball will show through.

4. To start with, work in rounds of crystals, working down the bauble. You can attach a few rounds in one colour and then switch to a new colour when you want.

5. Keep working until the whole bauble is covered with crystals apart from a very small 7–10mm gap at the top. Leave the glue to dry for several hours or overnight.

6. Cut a piece of ribbon for your loop and glue the ends in place in the 7–10mm gap you left. For added security use 2 pins to fasten the ribbon-ends into the bauble. Cover the pins and ribbon-ends with a few more crystals.

7. Leave to dry thoroughly before hanging on the tree.

Tip 1:

If the crystals start to slip in the glue as you are working, push the crystals back into place and dry the glue with a hairdryer. It can be helpful to do this after every couple of rounds.

Tip 2:

For added sparkle and a really high quality finish, you can always buy Viva12 or Swarovski crystals, which are a little more expensive, but will sparkle more than standard rhinestones.

POMPOM SNOWBALLS

Fluffy and furry puffs of fun to prettify your tree!

Tools and Materials:

- Red double knit (DK) yarn
- White double knit (DK) yarn
- Piece of card
- Pencil
- Scissors

Making pompoms with scraps of wool was one of the first craft projects I remember attempting as a child. These festive versions take me back to those days and make for a fluffy creative project to quickly fill the branches of your tree with little woolly cuddles. I find these are best made in front of the TV – feet up, whilst watching a suitable Christmas film! "

Susan

Instructions

1. Draw a circle onto a piece of card using a pencil and something circular like a small cup as your guide. The size of this circle will determine the size of your pompom. Draw a smaller second circle within the first.

2. Cut the shape out twice. You should end up with two matching 'doughnut-shaped' pieces of card.

3. Cut a length of red wool. Wind this around the two doughnut-shaped pieces of card. When you reach the end of your piece, tuck in the end and cut some more.

4. Continue until you have covered the card entirely with a layer of red wool.

5. Switch to the white wool and do the same – cover the doughnut-shaped card rings with a layer of white. Feel free to pause for a cup of tea at this stage – it can take a while!

6. Finally switch to the red again and keep winding until the red has covered the white completely.

7. Slide the tip of the scissors in between the two pieces of card and snip along the edges, cutting through all the strands of wool. Your pompom begins to appear…

8. Cut a 20cm length of wool and tie this around the pompom, between the two pieces of card. Pull tight and tie in a knot to secure.

Continued on next page...

Tip:

Try using just white wool for a proper snowball-effect pompom. Or use up some scraps of wool that have gathered from other projects – a seasonal rainbow combination of colours can also work and add a little vibrancy to your tree!

POMPOM SNOWBALLS

9. To make the hanging loop, cut 9 pieces of wool to a 30cm length (red, white or a mixture). Tie a knot at the top and divide the strands into 3 groups of 3. Ask a friend to hold the end, or use tape, and then plait the three groups of wool strands together to form one long plait. (**To plait:** pass the right group over the middle, then the left over the middle, repeat to end.) Knot the two ends together to form a loop.

10. Tie your plaited loop in place using the white strand of wool that is secured along the centre of your pompom.

11. Carefully remove the two pieces of card by cutting or tearing them away.

12. Puff out your pompom to make it fluffy and trim off any straggly ends of wool using your scissors to neaten. Then your cuddly, fluffy pompom is ready to hang!

Did You Know?

Christmas trees generally take 6–8 years to mature.

Christmas Beads (p. 12–13)

BAUBLES WITH RIBBON

Luscious ribbon-covered baubles to add a little class to your tree.

Tools and Materials:

- Foam ball(s)
- Clear glue
- Ribbon pieces
- Gold thread
- Scissors

Instructions

1. Select your first piece of ribbon and cut to size (it should reach from the top of your bauble to the bottom only). Cover the wrong side of this piece of ribbon with a thin layer of clear glue and stick to the foam ball.

2. Choose a matching piece of the same ribbon and stick to the opposite side of the foam ball in the same way.

3. Then work around the bauble, section by section, sticking your ribbon strips on one by one.

4. Keep going until you have space for just one ribbon on each side remaining.

5. For the last space, cut a length of ribbon that will fit all the way around the bauble with extra length to tie a bow at the top. Glue the ribbon around and leave the ends to hang loose for now.

6. Cut a piece of gold thread to use as your hanging loop. Tie it into a loop and thread over one end of the ribbon so that it sits at the top of the bauble.

7. Then tie your bow at the top of the bauble (using the ends of the long strand of ribbon that you left hanging). Remember to secure the gold thread loop into it too.

8. When you have finished, you should be able to hang up the bauble using the loop of gold thread.

Tip:

Try not to use ribbon that is too thick because the edges won't lay down flat on the foam ball (due to its curved surface). Ribbon under 1cm wide is best.

Section 2

SEWING PROJECTS

Dig out your needles,
Unravel that thread,
Choose festive fabrics
In green, gold and red!

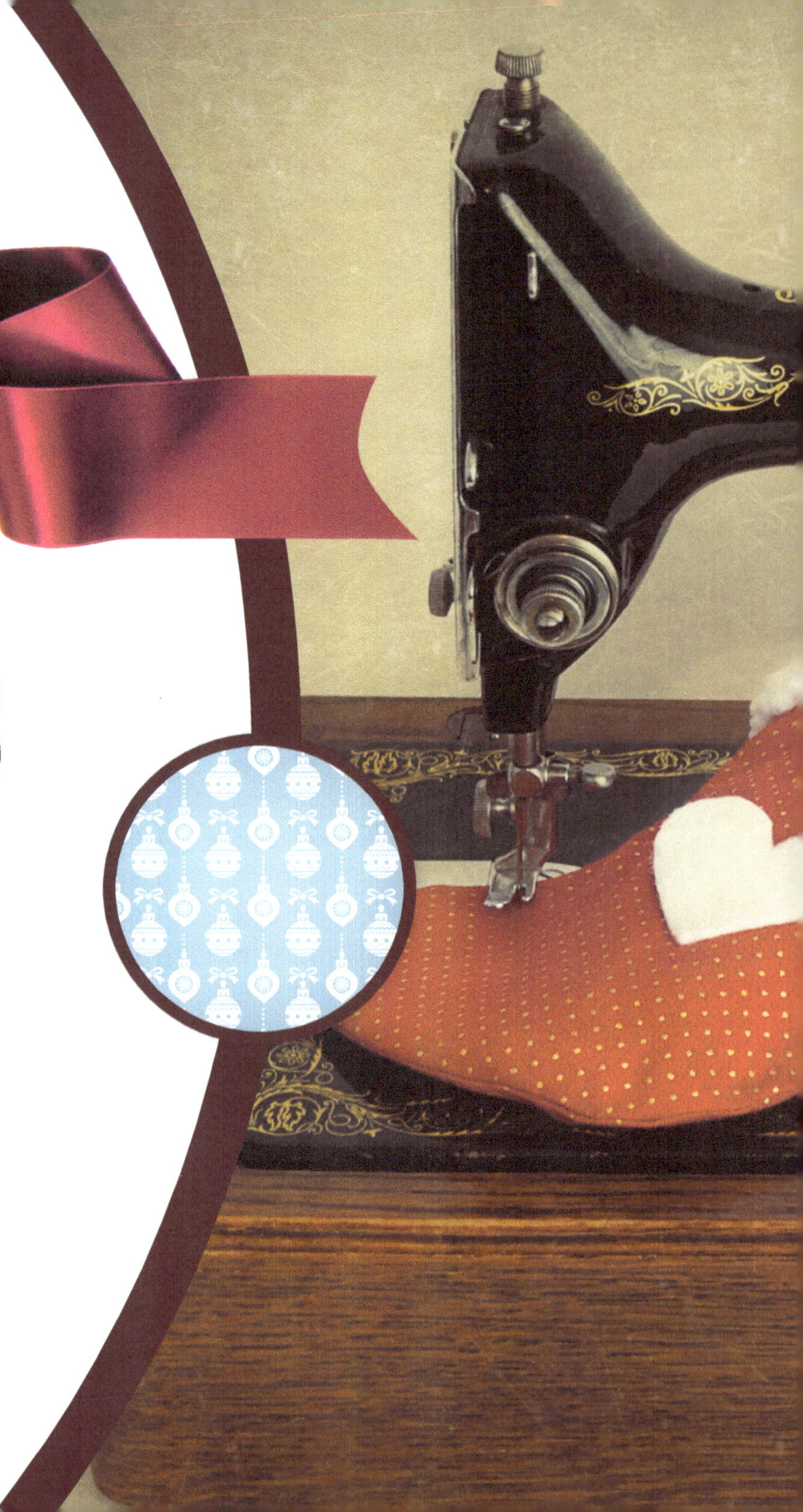

PATCHWORK STARS

Funky little stars that use up your Christmas scraps!

Tools and Materials:

- 30cm of 3–4mm ribbon and a wide ribbon scrap
- A selection of fabric scraps
- 1 large button
- Needle, pins and scissors
- Gold thread and plain thread
- Sewing machine
- Toy stuffing or wadding

'Every Christmas, as part of a regular sewing bee that I go to, we make each other a secret santa present out of a bag of scraps including fabric, ribbon, buttons and thread. Last year I was handed some gold thread, two small scraps of silk, a piece of wide ribbon and a large button... I was inspired!' *Susan*

Instructions

1. Copy and cut out the pattern pieces from the 'templates' section of this book and pin to your fabric scraps.

2. Cut out the shapes from your fabrics. Remember that the pattern already includes a 5mm seam allowance.

3. Load up your sewing machine with gold thread and sew a line of a fancy embroidery stitch of your choice down the centre of piece A. Sew on the large button and a scrap of ribbon to one point. Use photo 4 as a guide.

4. Join pieces B and C together using your sewing machine and where you have joined the pieces, sew over the top with a zigzag stitch in gold thread. Sew on piece D (the small star). Use photo 4 again as a guide.

5. Pin the two sides of the star together, right sides facing. Make sure that you enclose the 30cm of ribbon inside at the top point as your hanging loop.

6. Sew the pieces together on your sewing machine, allowing a 5mm seam allowance. Leave a 5cm gap on one side to turn the star through later on.

7. Trim off the excess fabric from the points of the star.

8. Turn it the right way around through the 5cm gap and stuff with toy stuffing until the star is completely full. Sew up the hole using matching thread and an invisible hand stitch. (See p.102 for help with this stitch.)

Tip:

To make sure that the points of your star are actually 'pointy' when you turn the star back through to the right side, use a blunt pencil or pointed object to push right into the corners and make them sharp.

FABRIC HEARTS

Select some fabric with Christmas patterns on for an adorable heart-shaped treat for your tree...

Tools and Materials:

- Christmas fabric(s)
- 15cm of 4–5mm ribbon for hanging
- Small button
- Toy stuffing (or wadding)
- Needle
- Thread
- Fabric scissors
- Pins
- Sewing machine

Instructions

1. Copy and cut out the heart pattern from the 'templates' section of this book.

2. Choose some Christmas fabric and find an area where you like the pattern. Draw around the pattern with a pencil. Cut out 2 heart shapes (front and back) leaving an extra 5–10mm of fabric for your seam.

3. Pin your two pieces right sides together ready to sew.

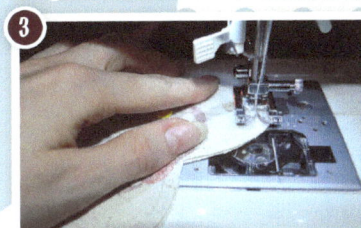 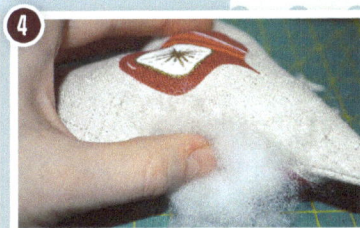

4. Using your sewing machine, set onto a straight stitch, sew along where your pencil line is to join the two hearts. Leave a 5cm gap at one edge. If you don't have a sewing machine you can always use hand stitching instead as the decoration is quite small. Trim off the excess fabric from the tip of the heart and make a small snip in the opposite end (between the two top pieces of the heart) to help the fabric sit better when you turn it the right way.

5. Turn the heart the right way around through the 5cm gap that you left. Use a blunt pencil or similar instrument to push the point of the heart as sharp as possible.

6. Fill the heart with some toy stuffing or wadding so that it is fully puffed out. Sew up the 5cm gap using small invisible stitches (i.e. catching each edge with a small hand stitch and work along).

7. Cut 15cm of ribbon using diagonal cuts so that the edges look neat. Form this into a loop and sew your button in place where the two ends of ribbon cross.

8. Sew this onto the top of your heart-shaped cushion with a few discrete hand stitches.

9. Hang on your tree or around the home!

Tip:

For something sweet-smelling, why not try filling these hearts with a little lavender or other yummy things such as cloves, cinnamon, herbs or potpourri?

GINGERBREAD MAN

A fun and felty version of the customary fairytale gingerbread man.

Tools and Materials:

- Light brown felt (1 x A4 sheet)
- 2–3 medium sized buttons
- 20cm of ribbon (1cm wide)
- Red embroidery thread
- White embroidery thread
- Toy stuffing (or wadding)
- 15cm of 3mm ribbon for loop
- 2 small beads
- Pencil
- Needle
- Scissors
- Pins

"Dating back to the 15th century and with plenty of popular fairytale stories surrounding them, these fun, easy-to-make gingerbread men are great for kids and adults alike. My felt-based version here will stand the test of time and can re-appear every year on your tree. Make one or make several – but remember, as good as they look, these are not for eating!"

Susan

Instructions

1. Copy and cut out the gingerbread man pattern from the 'templates' section of this book.

2. Fold your A4 sheet of brown felt in two and pin the paper pattern to the front, going through both layers.

3. Cut around your pattern so that you have 2 identical 'man-shaped' pieces of brown felt. One is the front and one the back.

4. Using a pencil, mark on the front piece of your gingerbread man where you want the eyes, mouth and buttons to go. You can copy the colours and design of our gingerbread man in the example here or use your own design.

5. Using some red embroidery thread (2 strands), use a couple of stitches to sew the eyes (2 small beads) in place, securing the end of the thread at the back of the felt (which will be the inside of the decoration).

6. Using the red embroidery thread (2 strands), and a simple back stitch, sew the smile of your gingerbread man using your pencil mark as a guide, again securing the ends of the thread at the back of the felt.

7. Tie a bow with the piece of ribbon you have chosen and sew this in place with a couple of stitches around his neck. Cut the ends of the ribbon diagonally to look pretty.

8. Finally, sew your 2–3 buttons in place along his tummy and the front of your gingerbread man is prepared!

Continued on next page...

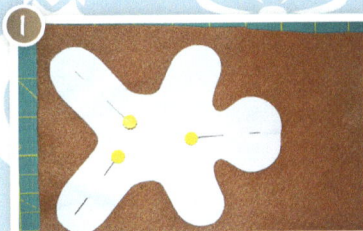

Tip:

Spend some time arranging your beads and buttons before you start sewing to achieve a good design. This is the fun part, where he begins to come to life! You can build some real character into your gingerbread man by using mis-matching buttons, ribbon or beads. Try changing the way that he smiles or maybe frowns! You could even make him a Santa hat!

GINGERBREAD MAN

9. Cut 15cm of thin ribbon (your hanging loop) and sew the two ends to the wrong side of the back piece of felt at the top of the head.

10. Place the decorated front on top of the back piece of felt that has the hanging loop attached, i.e. wrong sides are together enclosing all your stitches. Nearly there....

11. With the two pieces of felt lined up next to each other, sew a blanket stitch (see p.102) around the edge of your felt to join the two pieces together securely. Use 3 strands of the thread for a slightly thicker stitch and work in approx. 4–5mm stitches, keeping them as even and regular as you can.

12. Before you get all the way around the edge, stuff the inside with a small amount of toy stuffing or wadding to fill him out slightly.

13. Finish the remaining few stitches, cast off your thread and your seasonal gingerbead man is alive and kicking!

Did You Know?

One of the most famous Christmas trees is the tree in Trafalgar Square in London, which is given to the UK by Norway every year as a thank you present for the help the UK gave Norway in World War II.

CHRISTMAS PUDDING

A felt-based decoration good enough to eat!

Tools and Materials:

- Light brown felt (1 x A5 sheet)
- 15cm x 15cm white felt
- 5cm x 5cm dark green felt
- 3 small red beads
- 15cm of ribbon (3mm wide) for hanging
- White embroidery thread
- Toy stuffing (or wadding)
- Needle
- Fabric scissors
- Pins

Traditionally served on Christmas day as part of the Christmas dinner, the Christmas pudding (or plum pudding) is an inherent part of our festive tradition. Full of spices, dried fruit and treacle, decorated with holly or flaming brandy or maybe an added sixpence, no tree can miss out on having this crafty little version adorning its branches... "

Susan

Instructions

1. Copy and cut out the Christmas pudding patterns from the 'templates' section of this book.

2. Fold the A5 sheet of brown felt in two and pin the paper pattern for the pudding to the front. Cut around your pattern so that you have 2 identical pieces of brown felt.

3. Cut one piece of the 'cream' pattern from your white felt and two small holly leaves from the dark green felt. All your pieces are now ready to assemble!

4. Lay the white piece of felt on top of one of the brown pieces. Sew around the 'drippy' edges of the cream (in the centre of the decoration only) using small 2–3mm stitches. This secures the cream in place.

5. Cut 15cm of thin ribbon (your hanging loop) and sew the two ends to the wrong side of the back piece of felt at the top.

6. Place the decorated front on top of the back piece of felt that has the hanging loop attached i.e. wrong sides are together. With the two pieces of felt lined up, sew a blanket stitch (see p.102) around the edge of your pudding to join the pieces together. Use 3 strands of thread for a slightly thicker stitch and work in approx. 4–5mm stitches, keeping them as even and regular as you can.

7. Before you get all the way around the edge, stuff the inside with toy stuffing to fill out the pudding. Complete the remaining few stitches and cast off your thread neatly.

8. For the finishing touch, stitch the two small felt holly leaves in place at the top of the pudding and secure on the three small red beads to look like berries. Yum!

Tip:

For an added extra, why not enclose a small bell (from a toy or craft shop) into the inside of the pudding so that it 'rings' as if a sixpence was inside? Or hang it from the bottom of the decoration on a small piece of thread.

CHRISTMAS STOCKING

This Christmas stocking is perfect for filling with little presents and goodies ready for Christmas day!

Tools and Materials:

- Red Christmas fabric
- White Sirdar Snuggly 'snowflake' chunky yarn, 25g ball (Shade 0630)
- 4mm knitting needles
- 15cm of ribbon (3–5mm wide)
- 1 red medium-sized button
- Piece of white felt
- Tailor's chalk
- Needle and thread
- Iron
- Fabric scissors
- Pins
- Clear glue
- Sewing machine

"A mixture of sewing and knitting, this carefully crafted stocking is a combination of skills and perfect for hanging on your Christmas tree or on the mantelpiece this year, stuffed full of little gifts. " *Susan*

Instructions

1. Copy and cut out the stocking-shaped pattern from the 'templates' section of this book.

2. Select a piece of Christmas fabric and fold in half. Pin the pattern onto the fabric through both layers and draw around it with some tailor's chalk. Cut out your stocking shape using fabric scissors, leaving an extra 5–10mm of fabric for your seam. You now have two identical pieces of fabric (mirror images of each other).

3. Remove the pattern and pin your two pieces of fabric right sides together. At the top turn over 1cm of fabric on both sides and pin in place. This will create a neat top to the stocking.

4. Using your sewing machine, sew along your tailor's chalk line to join the two pieces. Make a couple of snips at the top of the foot where the stocking curves inwards (this allows the curve to sit correctly when turned the right way).

5. Turn the stocking the right way around and press with an iron to make the edges sharp and neat. Put to one side.

6. Take your white, Snuggly wool and cast on 8 stitches to your 4mm needles. Knit 60 rows of plain stitch. This strip of white knitting should fit around the top of your stocking. Depending on the tension of your knitting you may need more or less rows, so check the length against the stocking top as you go along.

7. When the knitting is the correct length, cast off and sew in the ends of the wool. Sew the piece of knitting on to the top of the stocking using some white thread.

8. Now you can add any additional decorations. In this example I have cut a white heart out of felt using some scissors and simply glued it on to the front. I have then cut a length of ribbon as a hanging loop and sewn this to the inside of the stocking with a button sewn on to the top.

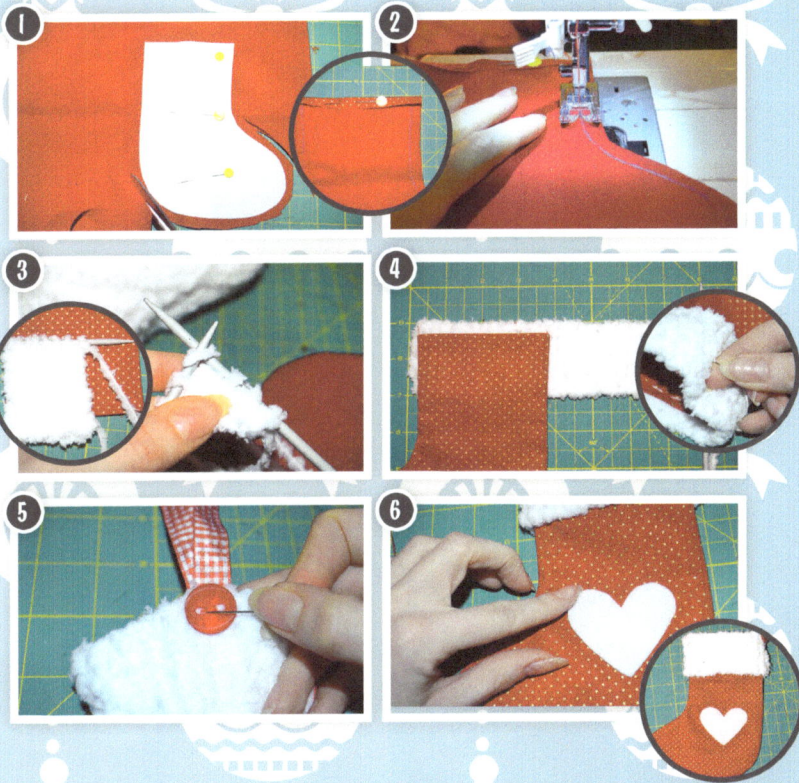

Tip:

Why not personalise your stockings by writing the name of each person on your pieces of white felt before gluing them on? You could also fill your stocking with gifts or little chocolates.

Mini Christmas Bunting

Tiny triangles of Christmas fun all linked together in a line…

Tools and Materials:

- A mixture of Christmas fabrics
- A mixture of Christmas buttons
- A mixture of Christmas ribbon
- Some red felt
- 2m length of 2–3cm red ribbon
- Tailor's chalk
- Needle
- Thread
- Rotary cutter
- Patchwork ruler (usually plastic)
- Pins
- Scissors
- Sewing machine
- Iron

Bunting is always one of my favourite decorations and this mini Christmas bunting is perfect for either draping all around your Christmas tree or pinning up around the home. It is also a great way to experiment with all the Christmas fabrics, buttons and ribbons you can find in shops around the festive season! **"** *Susan*

Instructions

1. Copy and cut out the triangle shape bunting pattern from the 'templates' section of this book.

2. Select a piece of Christmas fabric and fold it over so that you have an even number of layers (2, 4 or 6), depending on how many times you want to use your fabric in your design.

3. Place the triangle template over the layers of fabric and using a patchwork ruler and rotary cutter, cut out the triangle shapes, cutting through all layers of fabric as you roll the rotary cutter along your ruler. This is the quickest and most accurate way of creating many identical triangles for the bunting. Note: A 5mm seam allowance is already built into this pattern piece.

4. Choose another piece of fabric and again cut out 2,4 or 6 pieces using the pattern as a guide.

5. Continue using up all of your different fabric until you have enough pieces to make the length of bunting that you want. The example here is 15 triangles long, i.e. 5 different fabrics, each used 3 times (cut 6 pieces of each).

6. Pin two pieces of the fabric right sides together ready to sew. Continue pinning until all of the triangles are pinned together in pairs.

7. Using your sewing machine, find the 5mm guide on the bed of the machine and join the two pieces of fabric by sewing along only two sides. Leave the top (smallest) edge open and unsewn.

Continued on next page...

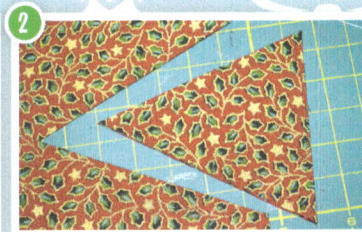

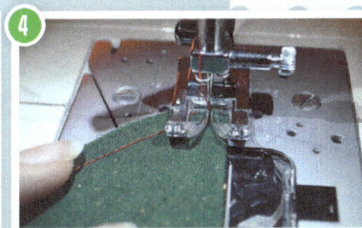

Tip:

You can make this bunting in a larger size as well. Create a triangle shape of your own or enlarge the pattern provided and follow the instructions in exactly the same way to make up a matching 'full size' strip of bunting to co-ordinate with your tree!

MINI CHRISTMAS BUNTING

8. Sew together all the triangles in the same manner using your sewing machine. Trim off the excess thread and the points of the triangles.

9. Turn all the triangles the right way around using a blunt pencil or similar object to make the points of the triangles sharp.

10. Press the triangles using an iron.

11. Take your length of ribbon and pin your first triangle to it, enclosing the top of the triangle in the ribbon. In other words you are encasing the rough edge of the triangle in the ribbon, which ends up being folded in half.

12. Measure 1 inch (2.5cm) along and attach the second triangle. Continue until all of your triangles are pinned in place. Try to mix up the fabrics into a combination that you like. This can be totally random or more carefully arranged.

13. Using your sewing machine, set on a zig zag stitch, sew all the way along the ribbon, removing the pins as you go, securing the triangles into the ribbon. Cast off and trim off the excess thread at the end.

14. You can either leave the bunting at this stage or, as in the example here, attach a mixture of Christmas buttons, pieces of ribbon and felt to the bunting. Place the buttons and ribbon in place on the individual pieces until you are happy with the arrangement and then sew on using small hand-stitches. Use the example here as a guide or create your own designs.

15. Trim the ends of the ribbon so that they are neat and your bunting is complete!

Did You Know?

Thomas Edison's assistants came up with the idea of electric lights for Christmas trees.

TARTAN TREES

A classic Scottish-themed tartan tree... for your tree!!

Tools and Materials:

- Small piece of tartan fabric
- 2 medium sized buttons
- 15cm of ribbon (3–5mm wide)
- Toy stuffing (or wadding)
- Tailor's chalk
- Needle
- Thread
- Fabric scissors
- Pins
- Sewing machine

I love a bit of tartan at Christmas and there are so many different tartan patterns that you can pick from when selecting your fabric for this decoration. Subtle, simple and classy, these soft little triangle-shaped trees are a great addition to your festive home-decorations!

Susan

Instructions

1. Copy and cut out the triangle-shaped tree pattern from the 'templates' section of this book.

2. Select your piece of tartan and fold in half. Pin the pattern onto the fabric – I always line up the tree with the straight lines of the tartan design but you can lay it out however you want.

3. Draw around the pattern, marking the fabric using some tailor's chalk. Cut out the tree using fabric scissors, leaving an extra 5–10mm of fabric for your seam. You now have two identical tree-shaped pieces of fabric. Pin your two pieces of fabric right sides together ready to sew.

4. Cut a 15cm loop of ribbon and pin it so that the loop is sandwiched in between the two right sides of the fabric.

5. Use your sewing machine to sew along the tailor's chalk line and join the two trees. Leave a 5cm gap at one edge. Trim off the excess thread and the excess fabric from the very top point of the tree. Check here that your ribbon is also securely fixed into place by the stitches as well.

6. Turn the tree shape the right way around through the 5cm gap. Use a blunt pencil to push the tip of the tree as sharp as possible.

7. Fill the tree with some toy stuffing or wadding.

8. Sew up the 5cm gap using small invisible stitches (i.e. catching each edge with a small hand stitch and work along until the gap is closed).

9. Sew the two buttons in place at the centre of the tree, one on either side. Use photo 6 as a guide. The stitches go all the way through the decoration, so it can help to choose buttons that are the same size and shape, with the same number of holes in them! Cast off your thread and you are all done!

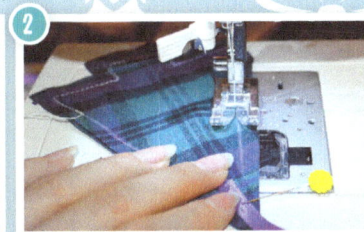

Tip:

Why not make a series of 8 or 10 of these trees on small 2cm loops? Then you can hang these on a piece of ribbon for a tree-shaped strip of bunting to hang up in your home!

43

CHRISTMAS ROBIN

A hand-stitched festive robin redbreast to perch on the branches of your tree.

Tools and Materials:

- Brown patterned cotton fabric
- Red patterned cotton fabric
- 2 small beads for eyes
- Red embroidery thread
- Toy stuffing (or wadding)
- Tailor's chalk
- Needle
- Thread
- Fabric scissors
- Pins

> This cute little hand-stitched robin decoration is a great way to use up small scraps of patterned patchwork fabric. You could even use a Christmassy red pattern for his tummy if you have it! He can be a little fiddly to construct due to the four-piece pattern, and his small size, so I would recommend stitching by hand rather than using the sewing machine to maintain accuracy in the shape. "
>
> *Susan*

Instructions

1. Copy and cut out the three pattern pieces from the 'templates' section of this book: 'side', 'top/bottom' and 'wing'.

2. Select a piece of brown patterned cotton and fold in half. Pin the 'side' shaped pattern onto the fabric, draw around with a tailor's chalk leaving a 5–10mm seam allowance.

3. Cut out the two pieces using fabric scissors. Check here that you have two pieces that are mirror images of each other (one for each side of the robin).

4. Select the 'top/bottom' pattern piece and repeat the two steps above but cutting out one piece in brown and one in a patterned red fabric.

5. You now have the 4 pieces of fabric ready to sew together to create the robin's body.

6. Take your two small beads, and sew in place on the two 'side' pieces of brown fabric to create the eyes.

7. Pin one of the 'side' pieces to the bottom piece using some pins and the chalk marks as a guide and making sure that the right sides of the fabric are together. Because we are pinning curves and constructing a 3D shape, it can be a little tricky at times to line up accurately.

8. Once pinned, use some small hand-stitches to sew the two sides together using your chalk lines as a guide.

Continued on next page...

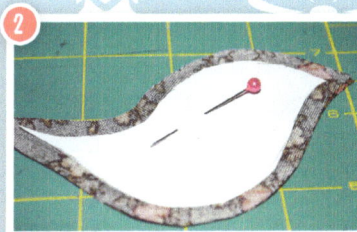

Tip:

Try creating this decoration in various colours and patterns! It is amazing to see the difference in your robin's character by altering the colour combinations. You can also try enlarging the pattern slightly to make him a little bigger – this makes him easier to construct too!

CHRISTMAS ROBIN

9. Join and sew the second side to the body.

10. Finally, pin the red patterned piece (the tummy side) to the three constructed pieces and stitch these together leaving a 3cm gap at one point. Make sure that where the four pieces of fabric join at the tail and beak that the point is sharp to create a good clean shape.

11. Turn the robin the right way around through the 3cm gap that you left. Use a pencil or other blunt tool to push the beak and tail into sharp points at either end.

12. Stuff the robin with some toy stuffing or wadding to fill him out.

13. Sew up the 3cm gap using some small invisible stitches.

14. Cut out four 'wing' shapes from your brown fabric (using the pattern provided), each with a seam allowance of 5mm added. Two of the pieces need to be mirror images of the other two, so it is easier to cut out from a folded piece of fabric.

15. Pin two of the pieces right sides together and sew along the chalk marks to join. Leave a small gap to turn the piece the right way around through. Once you have turned through, sew up the gap using small invisible stitches. Repeat to create a second wing.

16. Using a few small stitches, sew the two wings into place onto the sides of the robin. Try to keep the stitches underneath the wing so that they cannot be seen.

17. To finish, attach a loop of red embroidery thread to the top of the robin so he can hang on your tree.

Did You Know?

The tallest living Christmas tree is believed to be the 122-foot, 91-year-old Douglas fir in the town of Woodinville, Washington.

Section 3

FROM THE KITCHEN

Cinnamon, walnuts,
Oranges and dough,
Stick them together
And cover in snow...
Simple instructions,
Easy and quick,
Hang up on branches for
Good old St Nick...

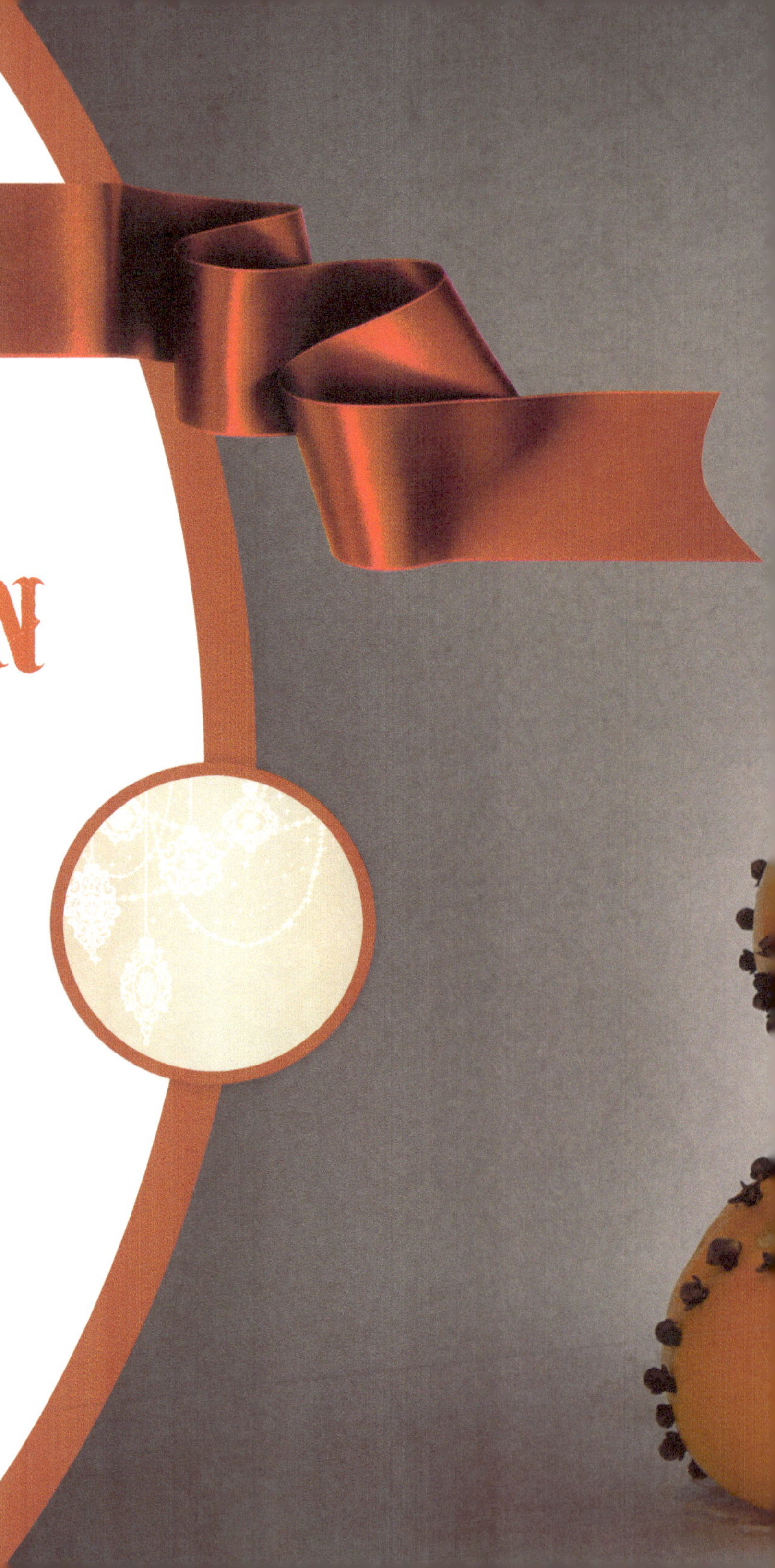

TRADITIONAL POMANDERS

Add a vintage twist to your tree with these classic clove-studded pomanders.

Tools and Materials:

Traditional Pomanders:
- Orange(s)
- Cloves
- Ribbon or gold string
- Glue (PVA or strong clear glue)
- Ground orris root, cinnamon and nutmeg (2 part orris root to 1 part of the other spices)

Carved Fruit (see p.52):
- Lime(s)
- Marker pen
- Linocutting tool
- Craft knife

I absolutely adore making pomanders. They look great, smell amazing and have a very homely and traditional Christmas look to them. They even work as fruity addition to a Christmas wreath, or you can place them fresh in a glass bowl or on your mantelpiece for a delicious smelling display! Just remember to start making these a few weeks before Christmas if you are drying them out for a long-lasting decoration. **Susan**

Instructions for Traditional Pomanders

1. Select a small orange or other citrus fruit and plan out a pattern that you would like to work with for your pomander design. Simple, bold lines and swirls work well. You can either use a pen to mark the skin of the fruit where you want to place the cloves or make it up as you go along!

2. Working carefully, begin to push the cloves individually into the skin of the orange. Traditionally, the cloves are placed right next to each other to help preserve the fruit for longer. Be careful not to break the cloves as you work. Keep going until your deign is compete but try to leave space for string or ribbon to wrap around and hang them up with.

3. Once the cloves are all inserted, roll your orange generously in the mixture of spices and orris root.

4. Leave the pomanders in a paper bag or box in a warm airing cupboard to dry out for 3-4 weeks or even at the bottom of a cool oven/aga for several days.

5. Once the pomanders are dried, select some ribbon (or gold string) and tie this around the orange, creating a bow and a loop at the top to hang it up with. You can secure the ribbon with glue if need be.

Tip:

If you find pushing the cloves into the orange skin hard on your fingers, punch holes into the skin first using a thick darning needle or skewer.

CARVED FRUIT DECORATIONS

Linocut into limes for a refreshing citrus-scented Christmas!

Instructions for Carved Fruit Decorations

1. Select a lime with a smooth dark green skin. The darker the green, the more the white cuts will stand out.

2. Using a marker pen, draw onto the skin a design that you would like to carve. Do keep the pen marks quite bold – bands of lines, stripes, spots, stars and swirls all work well.

3. Using a linocutting tool begin to carve into your lime. Work away from your fingers and take small strokes just a few millimetres deep and wide. If you are an avid printmaker (like me!) you may have a range of tools available to you to make different sized lines. If not, a craft knife can be used instead to carve your marks.

4. As with the traditional pomanders, when the carving is complete, leave them in a warm airing cupboard to dry out for several weeks or even in a cool oven/aga for several days

5. With the carved fruits, you can either wrap ribbon right around the fruit to hang it or just glue on some ribbon and gold string at the top, leaving a loop for hanging in the tree!

> " As an alternative to the clove-studded fruits, carving into the skin of oranges or limes can be a quirky alternative. The white pith of the fruit shows through and contrasts with the coloured skin for a pretty and eye-catching ornament. "
>
> *Susan*

Further Suggestions:

Once you have mastered traditional pomanders or carving into fruit, why not try combining the two? You can also decorate the pomanders with small nuts and seeds glued on and varnished to preserve them. Or try different citrus fruits such as grapefruit or lemon for different colours and shapes…

Make Your Own Mulled Wine

Why not use one of your fresh orange pomanders to spice up some wine whilst you create decorations in the kitchen!

Drop a pomander (just the orange with cloves inserted into it), some cinnamon sticks, 2oz sugar, 2 bay leaves, some grated nutmeg into a bottle of red wine, heat gently and serve…

DRIED FRUIT DECORATIONS

Have a Happy Christmas with these warming winter slices!

Tools and Materials:

- Oranges
- Knife
- Clear glue
- Thin ribbon (3–5mm wide)
- Selections of buttons
- Selection of beads
- Gold thread

With slices of dried orange as the starting point, these natural decorations are a chance to create some lovely hand-made tree ornaments. In this example, 3 different ways of using the fruit slices have been explored. Each one is demonstrated separately. "

Susan

Instructions

1. You can either purchase slices of dried orange from a craft supplier or dry out the fruit yourself.

2. To dry the fruit, start by slicing an orange into 3–5mm slices. Place on a baking tray and dry out in a cool oven (approx. 100-150°C) for 3–4 hours. Leave to cool before using.

Decoration 1

1. Choose a single slice of dried orange. Make a hole in the centre, large enough to thread the ribbon through.

2. Cut a suitable length of 3mm wide ribbon. Begin to wind this around the decoration passing through the centre hole, using the photos as a guide. Then take a length of thick gold thread and wind this around the fruit as well, over the top of your ribbon.

3. Use the ends of the ribbon and the gold thread at the top to create a hanging loop and a bow.

Continued on next page...

Tip:

If you like the look of the fruit exactly as it is, you can simply string these up onto your tree directly using some brown string or raffia ribbon. Or create a garland of dried mixed fruits.

Dried Fruit Decorations

Decoration 2

1. Select 2 slices of dried orange and glue them together using the photos as a guide.

2. Using some clear glue, stick a Christmas button or small decoration on the front of one of the orange slices. Again use the photos as a guide

3. Cut a 15cm strip of 3mm wide ribbon and glue this in a loop to the back of the decoration.

4. Leave to dry and then hang on your tree!

Tip:

These three decorations are just a starting point for how to use the dried orange slices. You could try drying lime, apple, pear or grapefruit slices as well or even different combinations of fruit, cinnamon, seeds, ribbon or beads as you become more confident with your making skills.

Decoration 3

1. Select 2 slices of dried orange. Make sure they are different sizes: small and large.

2. Glue some Christmas ribbon around the edges of the slices and leave to dry. Use the photo on p.57 as a guide.

3. String the slices up onto some gold thread. Tie knots on the string and use beads to stop the orange slices from falling off. Tie a loop at the top of the string so that the decoration will hang on the tree.

Did You Know?

Approximately 25–30 million real Christmas trees are sold each year in the United States. Almost all of these come from Christmas tree plantations.

SALT DOUGH SHAPES

Step into Christmas with a project the whole family can enjoy!

Tools and Materials:

- Plain flour
- Salt
- Water
- Mixing bowl
- Chopping board or kitchen surface
- Spoon
- Cup for measuring
- Rolling pin
- Cookie cutters in various shapes
- Acrylic paint & paintbrushes
- Skewer
- Clear varnish
- Baking tray & tin foil

One of my first forays into craft (aged 13) was making and then selling salt dough models at craft fairs. For these next two projects, I have revisited the craft to make some hand-crafted dough decorations for the tree. These are a great project for kids as well. Simple, safe and easy to get stuck in!

Susan

Instructions

1. Make up the salt dough mixture using the following measures: 2 cups flour, 1 cup salt, 1 cup water.

2. Pour all the ingredients into a mixing bowl and stir until they begin to form a dough.

3. Once the mixture is dough-like, use your hands to knead the dough and then shape it onto into a ball. You are then ready to create your shapes!

4. Using a rolling pin, roll out the dough onto a chopping board until it is around 4-5mm thick. Use flour underneath the dough to prevent it from sticking to the surface of the chopping board and your rolling pin.

5. Select a cookie cutter and press it into the dough to cut out your decoration. Stars, trees, bells, baubles, snowmen... any Christmas-related shape will do!

6. Keep going until you have used up all your dough and made several decorations.

7. Using a skewer, or other pointed utensil, make a small hole at the top of each decoration around 5mm from the edge.

8. Place the shapes on a baking tray and cook in the oven for 2–3 hours on a low heat, e.g. 110–130°C.

Continued on next page...

Tip:

Salt dough decorations will last for years as long as they are stored in a cool, dry and well ventilated area. If any water or damp gets near them, they will go soft and turn back into dough!

SALT DOUGH SHAPES

9. Keep an eye on the decorations whilst they cook: they shouldn't change colour, rise or burn. The heat simply dries them out until they are solid.

10. Remove from oven and leave to cool.

11. Using some acrylic paint, decorate the shapes with whatever colours and patterns you fancy. Remember to paint the back of the decoration as well as the front.

12. Leave the paint to dry.

13. Coat each decoration thoroughly with a layer of clear varnish to seal and protect.

14. Leave for 24 hours to dry. You will probably need to coat one side, leave to dry and then coat the other side.

15. Thread a piece of string through the hole at the top and hang on your tree or give as a gift to friends and family!

SALT DOUGH PHOTO FRAMES

Personalised, hand-made mini photo frames.

Tools and Materials:

- Plain flour
- Salt
- Water
- Mixing bowl
- Chopping board or kitchen surface
- Spoon
- Cup for measuring
- Rolling pin
- Cookie cutters in various shapes
- Acrylic paint & paintbrushes
- Skewer
- Clear varnish
- Baking tray & tin foil

Building upon the simple salt dough shapes made in the previous project, these mini picture frames are a perfect gift for Christmas. They are small personalised photo frames using your own pictures and photos – pop them straight onto the tree for something unique and special this year. ,, *Susan*

Instructions

1. Make up the salt dough mixture using the following measures: 2 cups flour, 1 cup salt, 1 cup water.

2. Pour all the ingredients into a mixing bowl and stir until they begin to form a dough.

3. Once the mixture is dough-like, use your hands to knead the dough and then shape it into a ball.

4. Using a rolling pin, roll out the dough onto a chopping board until it is around 3–4mm thick. Use flour underneath the dough to prevent it from sticking to the surface of the chopping board and your rolling pin.

5. Select a circular or star-shaped cookie cutter and press it into the dough to cut out the back of the photo frame.

6. Using a skewer, make a hole at the top of this back part of the frame (for hanging later on).

7. Cut out a second identical shape for the front piece of the frame.

8. Using a smaller cutter (the same shape), cut out the centre of the frame on this front piece. The front piece now looks like a frame.

9. Keep going until you have used up all your dough and cut out the elements for several decorations. Stars, squares, ovals and circles work well for these frames.

Continued on next page...

Tip:

When making your frames, you can always cut the dough using a knife if you don't have cookie cutters available. You can also make marks into the dough using knives, forks or cocktail sticks if you want to add some texture. Glitter, sequins and other decorations can also be glued on top of your painting too…. Get creative with it!

SALT DOUGH PHOTO FRAMES

10. Place the fronts and backs of your frames on a baking tray and cook in the oven for 2–3 hours on a low heat e.g. 110–130°C.

11. Remove from oven and leave to cool.

12. Using some acrylic paint, decorate the back of the decoration with whatever colours and patterns you fancy. Remember to paint the edges of the decoration as well. Leave the paint to dry.

13. Using the same paint and pattern, paint the front part of the frame to match. Again, leave to dry.

14. Finally, coat the fronts and backs of your frames thoroughly with a layer of clear varnish to seal and protect. Leave for 24 hours to dry.

15. Thread a piece of string through the hole at the top of the back piece of the frame.

16. Select a photo you want to place into the frame and cut to size. Use the cookie cutter or the decoration itself as a guide. Aim to cut the photo to around 3–5mm smaller than the very edge of the frame.

17. Using a thin layer of glue, stick the photo to the back part of the frame (the solid / unpainted side).

18. Using a layer of glue all around the edge of the frame, glue the front of the frame to the back piece that has the picture stuck to it. Leave to dry fully.

19. They are ready to give as gifts to friends and family!

WALNUT WONDERS

A wonderful 'walnutty' addition to your tree this year…

Tools and Materials:

- Bag of walnuts
- Gold spray paint
- Small beads
- Clear glue
- Gold thread
- 3mm wide ribbon or cord
- Scrap newspaper

Instructions

1. Lay down some scrap newspaper on a table, or the floor, and place the walnuts in the centre of it.

2. Following the instructions on the can of spray paint (i.e. keeping the can at least 20cm away from the object), begin to coat the walnuts with a light coating of gold on one side.

3. Leave the walnuts to dry for 45 minutes and then turn them over to spray the other side so that the walnuts are completely coated in gold. Again leave them to dry fully.

4. Once dry, you can start to decorate the gold-coated walnuts even more! Try arranging ribbon, beads or even small seeds around the sides of the walnuts to see what it looks like before sticking them on.

5. Apply some clear glue to the walnut where you want to apply the ribbon or beads. Then carefully stick your items into the clear glue and allow to dry before moving to the next stage.

6. Create a loop with a piece of gold thread and tie a knot to secure it. Keep this handy.

7. Glue a longer strip of ribbon all around the walnut and then tie the two ends at the top in a bow, securing your gold loop of thread into it as you go.

8. Hang on your tree!

Tip:

If you hold the spray paint too close to the surface of the walnut or use too much, the gold paint can drip down the side of the walnut.

Alternative:

Try using silver spray paint instead of gold if this suits the colour scheme on your tree a litte better!

CINNAMON BUNDLES

Fragrant little bundles of cinnamon sticks.

Tools and Materials:

- Packet of cinnamon sticks
- Clear glue
- Gold thread
- Christmas ribbon

Cinnamon always reminds me of Christmas as it is used so often in yummy recipes for cakes and mulled wine! So why not buy a little extra this year and display some on your tree as well? **"** *Susan*

Instructions

1. Select 4–5 cinnamon sticks to use per decoration.

2. Bundle the sticks together on top of each other. Use the photos as a guide.

3. Glue the sticks together using clear glue. To do this run a line of glue along one cinnamon stick and press the next one against it. Repeat until your bundle is stuck together.

4. Make as many bundles as you want and leave them all to dry completely.

5. Cut a length of ribbon and wrap around your bundle of cinnamon sticks, tying a bow at the top.

6. If you have a strip of lace you can layer this up with some thinner ribbon to create a slightly different effect.

7. You can either tie a loop of string into the bow to hang the bundle from or use the ribbon itself to create a hanging loop.

8. ...and your bundles are complete!

Tip:

It is a good idea to lay out your bundles and tie them up without the glue first to see whether you like the combinations of ribbon that you have selected.

LET'S GET CREATIVE

Gifts to inspire a winter's day?

'Let's get creative' I hear you say!

With simple white snowflakes

And modelling clay,

There's plenty to crochet,

Craft, make and play!

CROCHET BAUBLES

A stripy, super-soft special crochet project...

Abbreviations:

dc = double crochet   ch = chain   st = stitch
ss = slip stitch   dc2tog = double crochet 2 together

Note: For explanations of crochet stitches please see p.102–103

Tools and Materials:

- 3.5mm crochet hook
- Two different colours of double knit yarn
- Scissors
- Darning needle
- Toy stuffing or wadding
- Stitch marker (optional)

These quick-to-make baubles are created using the Amugurumi style of crochet, i.e. mainly a double crochet stitch, worked in circles. This pattern starts at the bottom of the ball, increasing on each round to its widest part and then decreasing again to the top. **Susan**

Instructions

In this example, Yarn A is red and Yarn B is green. The two colours are worked alternately in a continuous line of double crochet that builds up the sphere as you go, i.e. no need to ss at the end of every round. Although it may appear more complex using more than one yarn, using two gives you clear visibility of the different rounds, which can be difficult to see clearly when working in one colour of yarn only.

To start: Yarn A, slip knot and 2ch
Rnd 1: Yarn A: 6dc into 2nd ch from hook
Rnd 2: Yarn A: 2dc into each dc = 12 dc
Rnd 3: Yarn B: [1dc, 2dc into next st] 6 times = 18dc
Rnd 4: Yarn A: [2dc, 2dc into next st] 6 times = 24dc
Rnd 5: Yarn B: [3dc, 2ch into next st] 6 times = 30dc
Rnd 6: Yarn A: 1dc in each st = 30dc
Rnd 7: Yarn B: 1dc in each st = 30dc
Rnd 8: Yarn A: 1dc in each st = 30dc
Rnd 9: Yarn B: 1dc in each st = 30dc
Rnd 10: Yarn A: 1dc in each st = 30dc
Rnd 11: Yarn B: [1dc in next 3st, dc2tog] 6 times = 24dc
Rnd 12: Yarn A: [1dc in next 2st, dc2tog] 6 times = 18dc
Rnd 13: Yarn B: [1dc in next st, dc2tog] 6 times = 12dc
At this stage stop to fill the bauble with toy stuffing or wadding.

To finish: dc2tog until the hole at the top closes. Secure the end with a ss and leave a long length of wool to use as a loop for hanging. Secure the end of the yarn and sew in.

Tip:
At the end of each round, count the total stitches to make sure you are keeping to the pattern. You can use a stitch marker to mark the rows as well – move the stitch marker to the last stich of every row as you work.

MODELLING CLAY DECORATIONS

Model three unique clay ornaments from scratch.

Tools and Materials:

- Green modelling clay
  (we use Fimo 38)
- Red modelling clay
  (we use Fimo 202)
- Brown modelling clay
  (we use Fimo 77)
- White modelling clay
  (we use Fimo 0)
- Plastic chopping board
- Knife
- Rolling pin
- Baking tray and tin foil

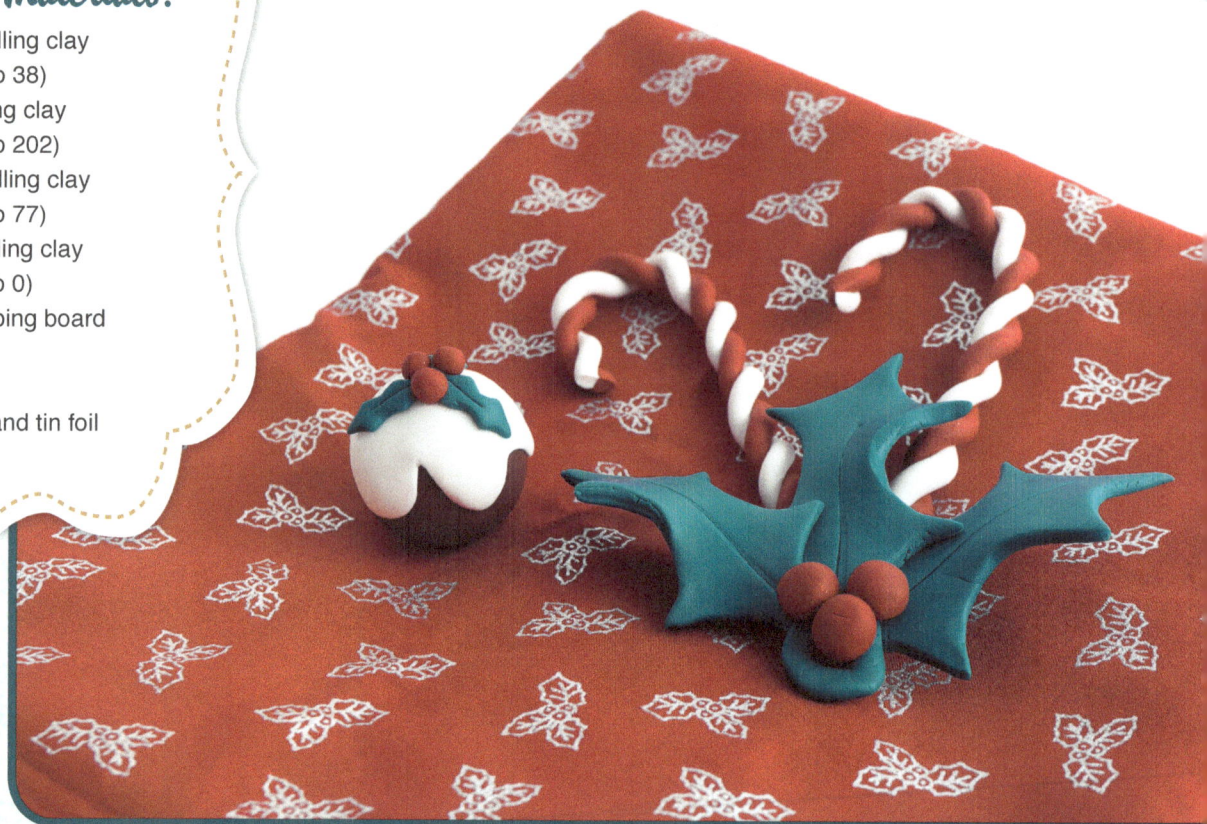

> *Modelling clay is perfect for creating unique Christmas shapes that can be strung up onto the tree. I have created three different examples here but once you have the clay, the possibilities are endless... Get modelling!* ,,
>
> *Susan*

Christmas Pudding Instructions

1. Take a lump of the brown modelling clay (Fimo) and warm up in your hands. Once the clay is warm, roll it into a round ball. This represents the 'pudding'. The size of this ball will determine how large your decoration is. In the example here, the pudding is 2.5cm (1inch) wide.

2. Warm up a smaller piece of white clay in your hands. This piece will be used to create the cream or brandy sauce on the top of the pudding, so it needs to be large enough to cover the top of the pudding and then wrap down the sides.

3. Flatten the white piece so that it is just a few millimetres thick. Make the edges rounded to look like thick gloopy cream. Wrap this piece over the top of the pudding and smooth down to secure in place**.**

4. Take a small piece of green clay, warm up and roll out flat. Using a knife, cut out three very small holly leaf shapes. Stick these on top of the pudding.

5. Roll out a three small 3mm balls of red Fimo and secure these on the top of the pudding to represent the holly berries. Try to leave a small space underneath the berries or holly to allow you to thread a piece of cotton later on to hang up.

6. Once your pudding is finished and all the pieces safely stuck together, place on a baking tray covered in tin foil ready to cook/harden. See p.78 for cooking instructions.

Tip:

Make sure you wash your hands and clean your chopping board between using different colours. The white clay in particular can become grubby quickly if it comes into contact with stained fingers!

Modelling Clay Decorations

Holly Leaves Instructions

1. Warm up a large piece of green clay in your hands. Roll this out onto the chopping board until it is about 2–3mm thick and large enough to cut out your shapes from. The holly leaves in this demonstration are around 5–6cm long and 2.5cm wide.

2. Using a knife cut out three holly leaf shapes. Use the photos as a guide. Using the knife, make a score down the centre of the leaves.

3. Arrange the three leaves together in a cluster on a baking tray pressing the leaves together at the top to secure them together. Again use the photo as a guide. You can use small rolled up balls of foil to place under the leaves to give them a bit of a 3D shape.

4. Take a small piece of the leftover green clay, roll into a thin sausage shape and create a loop at the top to hang the decoration from. This only needs to be big enough to pass a piece of string through.

5. Warm up some red Fimo and roll this into three small balls to create the berries. Place these on the holly leaves at the top and try to cover the hanging loop as you do so.

6. Place on a baking tray covered in tin foil ready to cook/ harden. See p.78 for cooking instructions.

> *Modelling clay is perfect for creating unique Christmas shapes that can be strung up onto the tree. I have created three different examples here but once you have the clay, the possibilities are endless... Get modelling!* **"** *Susan*

Candy Cane Instructions

1. Take a piece of white Fimo and warm up in your hands.

2. Roll this out on the chopping board into a long thin sausage shape. Roll it out as long as your chopping board and around 5mm in diameter.

3. Repeat with some red Fimo.

4. Place the two matching strips of Fimo on the chopping board next to each other.

5. Holding one end, wind the two pieces up so they wrap around each other into one stripy sausage shape. This begins to look like candy now – sugary and sweet!

6. Chop the strip to as long as you want your decoration to be. You should get a couple of decorations out of your long strip.

7. Lay the strip down into a baking tray and shape the end into a curve so that it looks like a candy cane.

8. Place on a baking tray covered in tin foil ready to cook/harden. See p.78 for cooking instructions.

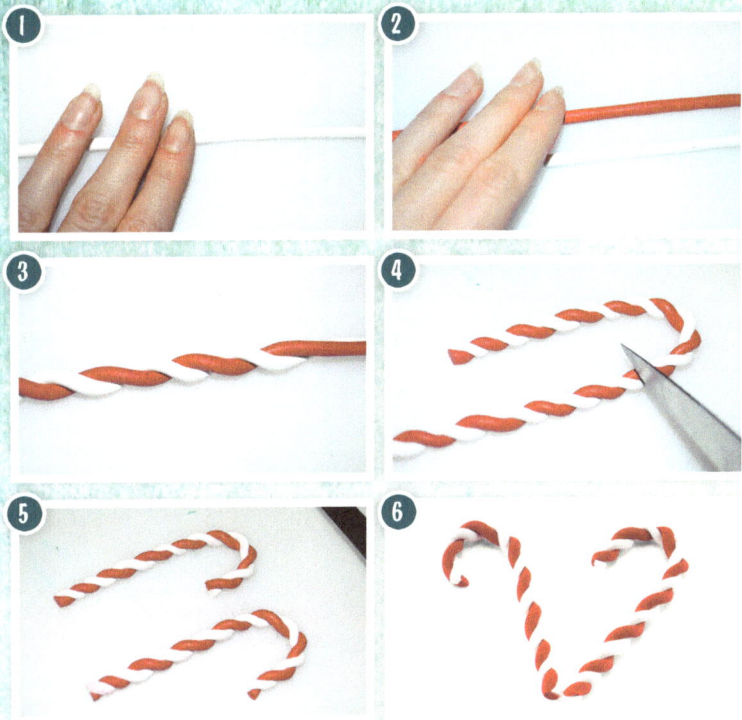

Tip:

The candy canes can hang on the tree exactly as they are with no need for string – once they have cooled down from the oven of course!

MODELLING CLAY DECORATIONS

Cooking Instructions

1. Preheat your oven to 100°C, i.e. a cool temperature or the temperature that is recommended on your packet of clay.

2. Place a sheet of tin foil over a baking tray.

3. Lay out all of your created Fimo models on the foil with a few centimetres gap between them. If you have made a lot of decorations, you may need a few trays!

4. Once the oven is warm, place the tray inside and cook the items for as long as is recommended on the packet of modelling clay. This is usually around 30mins.

5. Once the decorations have thoroughly hardened remove the tray from the oven.

6. Leave to cool for about an hour.

7. Once cool, thread thin white string through any models that need a hanging loop and place on the branches of your tree!

Did You Know?

The average Christmas tree contains
about 30,000 bugs and insects!

Modelling Clay Decorations (p.74–78)

CROCHET SNOWFLAKE

Create a woolly winter wonderland with this timeless addition to any tree.

Abbreviations:

dc = double crochet
tr = treble crochet
ss = slip stitch
htr = half treble

ch = chain stitch
dtr = double treble
trtr = treble treble

Note: For explanations of crochet stitches please see p.102–103

Tools and Materials:

- 3.5mm crochet hook
- Double knit wool in white
- Darning needle
- Scissors
- Pins
- Iron

"Suitable for beginners to advanced crochet fans, this easy to make snowflake explores several basic crochet stitches. The snowflake is created in the round and is a great little project to make in one sitting. Tension isn't important in this decoration – just try to make it consistent throughout." **Susan**

Crochet Instructions

Round 1: Slip knot to start, 6ch, ss into 1st ch to make a ring

Round 2: 1ch, 12dc into ring, ss into 1st ch at start of round

Round 3: 1ch, dc into same place as ch, [*7ch, miss 1dc, 1sc info next dc] repeat from * x5, 5ch, miss 1dc, 1htr into top of first dc

Round 4: 3ch (counts as 1tr), 4 tr into arch formed by 7ch, [*3ch, 5tr into next 7ch arch] repeat from * x5 3ch, ss into top of 3ch at beginning of round

Round 5: [*6ch, dc into 2nd ch from hook, 1 htr into next ch, 1 tr into next ch, 1dtr into next ch and 1 trtr into next ch, 5dc] repeat from * x5 ss to end

To finish: Sew in the ends using a darning needle. Attach a loop of wool to one of the points of the snowflake for hanging.

Blocking (for a crisp snowflake shape): Soak the snowflake in water and pin onto an ironing board so that all the points are evenly spaced. Leave to dry. Unpin and your snowflake is complete!

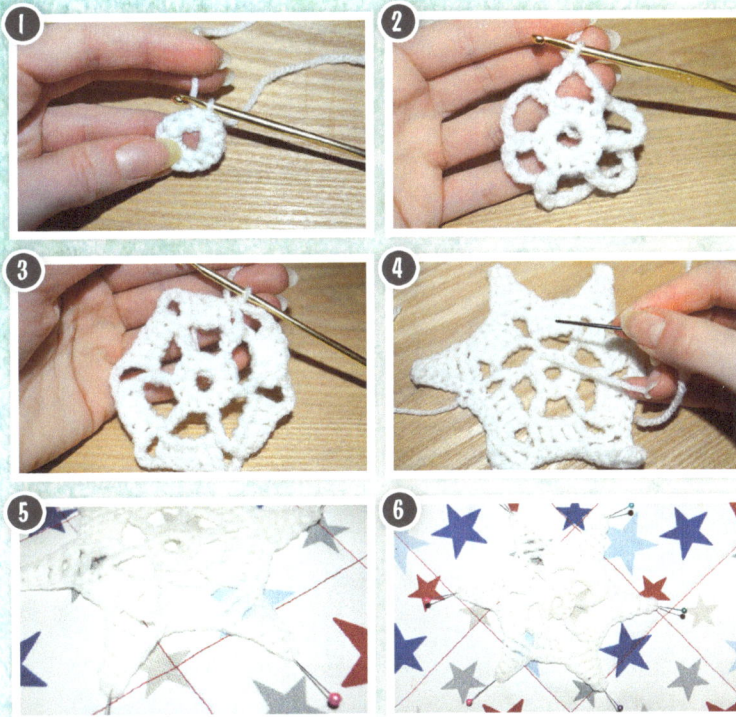

Key

•	ss
○	ch
✕	dc
T	htr
†	tr
‡	dtr
‡	trtr

Crochet Chart

Tip:

You can also make this snowflake using 4ply yarn and a 1.75mm crochet hook for a finer crochet stitch and smaller finished decoration.

CROCHET SNOWMAN

Frosty the friendly snowman!

Abbreviations:

dc = double crochet   inc = increase
ss = slip stitch   dec = decrease
ch = chain stitch   tr = treble crochet

Note: For explanations of crochet stitches please see p.102–103

Tools and Materials:

- 3mm crochet hook
- White double knit yarn (body)
- Red and pale green double knit yarn (for hat and scarf)
- Brown yarn (eyes)
- Darning needle
- Toy stuffing or wadding
- Stitch marker (optional)
- Scissors

Instructions (Body)

To start: Slip knot, ch2

Rnd 1: 6dc into 2nd ch from hook. Place the stitch marker on this last stitch and then move to the last stitch of each row as you progress up the body

Rnd 2: 2dc into each stitch = 12 stitches

Rnd 3: [1dc, inc] x 6 = 18 stitches

Rnd 4: [2dc, inc] x 6 = 24 stitches

Rnd 5: [3dc, inc] x 6 = 30 stitches

Rnd 6: [4dc, inc] x 6 = 36 stitches

Rnds 7-11: 36dc

Rnd 12: [4dc, dec] x 6 = 30 stitches

Rnd 13: [3dc, dec] x 6 = 24 stitches

Rnd 14: [2dc, dec] x 6 = 18 stitches

Rnd 15: [1dc, dec] x 6 = 12 stitches

Stuff body with toy stuffing

Rnd 16: [1dc, inc] x 6 = 18 stitches

Rnd 17: [2dc, inc] x 6 = 24 stitches

Rnd 18: [3dc, inc] x 6 = 30 stitches

Rnds 19-22: 30dc

Rnd 23: [3dc, dec] x 6 = 24 stitches

Rnd 24: [2dc, dec] x 6 = 18 stitches

Rnd 25: [1dc, dec] x 6 = 12 stitches

stuff head of snowman with toy filling

Rnd 26: dec to end until hole at top closes

To finish body: Double knot yarn to finish. Cut off excess yarn. Sew in ends of yarn using a darning needle

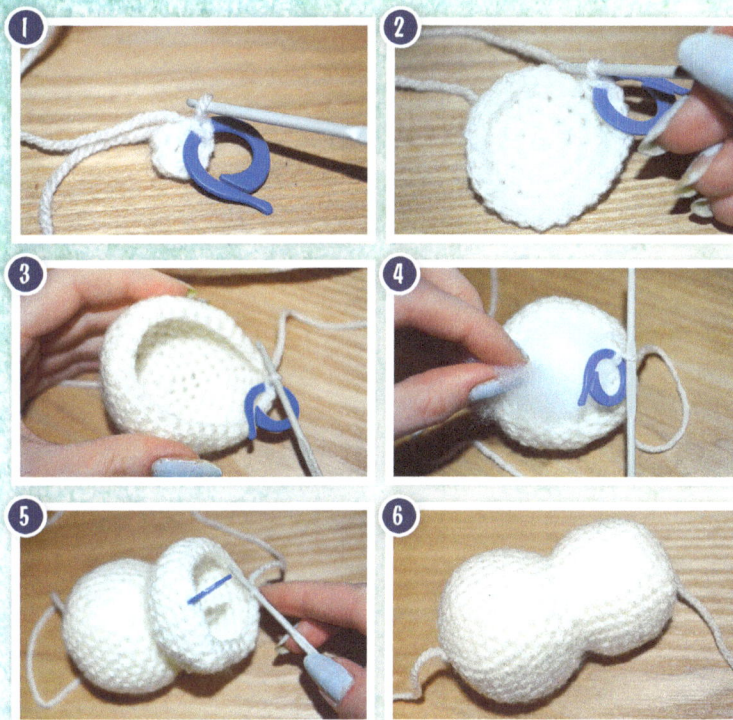

Tip:

When making Amigurumi style crochet toys, choose a hook just a little smaller than your yarn instructions say, i.e. if the yarn recommends a 4mm hook, try a 3.5 or 3mm hook intead. This is to make sure that the stitches are close together and no stuffing comes through the toy.

CROCHET SNOWMAN

Instructions (Scarf)

The scarf is worked in a straight row rather than in the round.

To start: Slip knot with the red yarn

Row 1: 38ch

Row 2: Start at the 2nd ch from the hook (i.e. 1st 2ch counts as a tr), 36tr

To finish: Double knot yarn and sew in loose ends to neaten. Attach the green yarn at the ends to create four tassels on each end (see photos). For the example here we have attached two strands of green yarn approx. 7cm in length for each tassel.

Instructions (Hat)

The hat is worked in the round, starting with the widest part (the brim of the hat) and working down to the point at the top.

Rnd 1: (**Green Yarn**) Slip knot, 30ch. ss to make a ring.

Rnd 2: (**Green Yarn**) 30dc (i.e. one dc into each stitch).

Rnd 3 onwards: (**Red Yarn**) [4dc, dec] repeat until there are just 8 stitches remaining. Then dec to end.

To finish: Leave a 15cm length of yarn at the end and make into a hanging loop by sewing in the end to the top of the hat. Double knot yarn and sew in end to secure.

To Assemble

1. Sew two eyes onto the face of the snowman by using the brown yarn and the photo as a guide. In the example here, this was done with around 4–5 stitches of 4mm in length. Using some red yarn and the same method as above, stitch two red buttons down the front of the body.

2. Tie the scarf around the neck. No need to sew in place, just tie it in a knot around the neck.

3. Place the pointy hat on his head, slightly towards the back of the head to show his face and sew in place using the red yarn and a needle.

Did You Know?

There are more than 10 different varieties of Christmas tree grown in the UK. The most common tree sold is now the Nordmann fir.

Crochet Snowman (p.82–84)

THRIFTY TREATS

Nifty and thrifty,
Cheap, fun and quick
These final five projects
Are made in a tick!

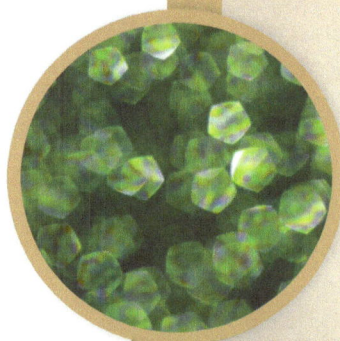

MINI PRESENTS

Cute little present boxes made from last year's Christmas cards!

Instructions

I. Choose a Christmas card with a good colour and pattern to use for the top of your box. If the card is rectangular in shape, cut it into a square instead, using scissors.

Tools and Materials:

- Selection of large Christmas cards
- White card
- Scissors
- Ribbon
- Ruler

"I first made these little Christmas present boxes when I was about 8 years old and for some reason the design has stuck with me ever since. These are a great way to use up last year's Christmas cards (which I just hate to throw away!) and only take 5 minutes to complete. Fill them with little gifts for an extra special ornament or leave them as purely decorative – the choice is yours! " *Susan*

2. Take your square, fold it in half diagonally, crease well and unfold. Fold diagonally the other way, crease and unfold.

3. Fold in one of the corners to the centre of the square.

4. Fold each of the remaining 3 corners in so that you end up with a smaller square and the 4 points all facing in to the centre of the square.

5. Fold one side of the square over to the centre and repeat on the other side. Use photo 5 as a guide. Crease well and unfold.

6. Repeat on the other sides. Crease well and unfold.

7. Unfold two of the corners and then snip along the two crease lines going towards the centre square (top of the box). Use photo 7 as a guide. Repeat on the other side so that you have made 4 cuts.

8. Leaving the two unfolded edges flat (the edges with the points at the end) fold up the two sides shaping the cut edges inwards to create two sides of the box.

9. Fold over the two flat sides to create the final two sides to the box. The top of your box is now complete.

10. Repeat the folding instructions with the square of white card (bottom of the box). This piece of card needs to be about 5mm smaller than the top.

11. Fill the box with a gift and construct so that the top goes over the bottom of the box. Tie a ribbon around it, to look like a present and hang on your tree!

Tip:

The size of these boxes will vary depending on the size of your starting piece of card. However the smaller the card, the harder these can be to fold into shape. Maybe try using plain card from a craft supplier or thick wrapping paper. Why not use some spare pieces of Christmas card as gift tags to label who your mini presents are for?

CHRISTMAS GOLD CONES

Glittery, gold cones that sit and sparkle on the branches of your tree.

Tools and Materials:

- Pinecones
- Gold spray paint
- Glitter glue
- Paintbrush or cotton bud
- Scrap newspaper
- Gold thread (optional)

Instructions

1. Lay down some scrap newspaper on a table or the floor and place the pinecones in the centre, on top of it. Work in a well-ventilated area or outside in the garden.

2. Following the instructions on the can of spray paint (i.e. keeping the can at least 20cm away from the cones), begin to coat them with a light coating of gold. It can be tricky to get inside the pinecones, so you may need to work in stages. Spray an area, leave to dry for 30mins and then return to continue.

3. Once dry, we can add a little silver glitter glue to the edges! Pour out some of your glitter glue onto a jam jar lid or scrap of card. Using a paintbrush or cotton bud apply a generous dollop of the glitter to the very ends of the pinecones. Leave to dry and your work here is done!

4. You can either rest the cones directly on the branches of the tree or tie a small piece of gold thread to the top of your cone and hang as if it were a bauble. These also work well as an addition to festive potpourri and wreaths!

FABRIC BUNDLES

Yummy bundles of Christmas magic…

Tools and Materials:

- Christmas fabric
- See-through gold/silver fabric
- Tailor's chalk or a pencil
- Cellophane
- Elastic or string
- Some chocolates
- Ribbon or sequined ribbon
- Plate
- Fabric scissors

> *These shiny decorations are a great way to display some sweets or chocolates on your tree. Easy to make and a handy way to use up scraps of fabric. You can make these year after year as decorations that also act as impromptu gifts for your visitors over the festive season!* **"**
>
> *Susan*

Instructions

1. Using tailors chalk and a small dinner plate, draw a circle onto the back of some patterned Christmas fabric.

2. Cut out the circle of fabric using your fabric scissors.

3. Cut out a circle of see-through or matching gold/silver fabric just 1cm larger than the first circle.

4. Cut out a square of cellophane at least 3–5cm larger than both your circles.

5. Layer these cut-outs so that you have the cellophane first, the see-through fabric second and the patterned Christmas fabric on top, all wrong sides up.

6. Place 2–3 chocolates or sweets in the centre of the layers. If the chocolates are not in wrappers, use a small off-cut of your cellophane to wrap the chocolates up first. This will keep them fresh whilst they hang on your tree.

7. Pull the edges of the fabric layers up and around the chocolates to create a bundle.

8. Secure this with some string or elastic. Leave a loop so that you can use it to hang up the bundle on the tree.

9. Decorate the bundle with some ribbon or sequined ribbon to cover the string.

10. Make some more and hang on your tree.

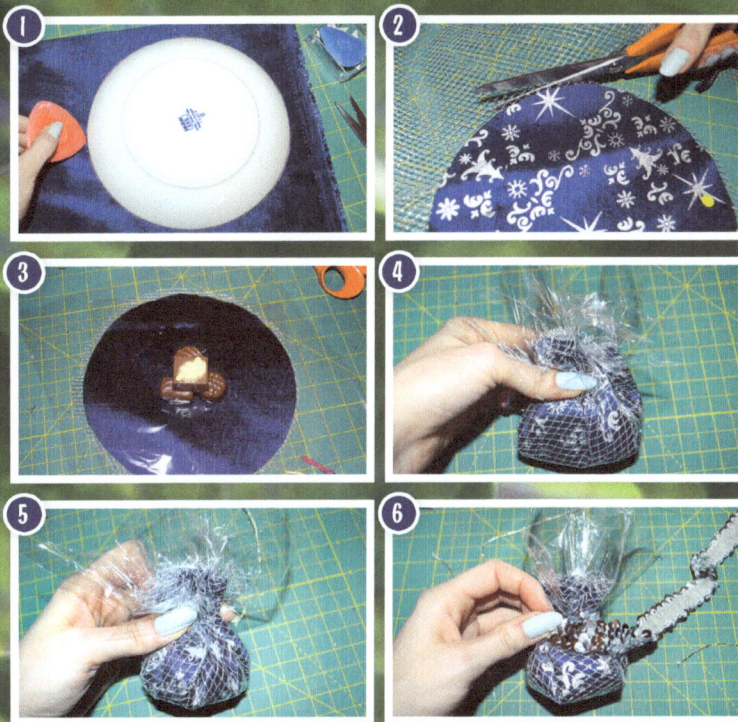

Tip:

Remember to keep the bundles away from any warm tree-lights if they have chocolates inside! Why not try using sweets or mini-gifts inside the bundles instead of chocolates?

BUTTONTASTIC WREATHS

Mini wreaths of button-based fun!

Tools and Materials:

- Selection of medium-sized buttons
- Thin wire (e.g. jewellery wire)
- Wire cutters or jewellery pliers
- Thread to hang

These quick-to-make, simple little circles of buttons are an alternative to a traditional wreath and you can produce them in various sizes and colours to match your tree. If you are anything like me and have jars of unused buttons around, this is a great way to put them to use. ,, *Susan*

Instructions

1. Tip out a selection of buttons on to your table and choose those that you want to use for your mini-wreath.

2. Arrange the buttons in a circle to try out your colour combinations before getting started.

3. Cut a length of jewellery wire twice the length that your wreath will be, plus an added 10cm for the hook. In this example the wreath is about 9cm across (approximately 70cm of wire used).

4. Fold the wire in half to make it thicker and stronger. Trim the ends to neaten.

5. Begin to string your buttons onto the wire by threading the wire through the holes in the centre of each button.

6. Continue until all the buttons are loaded on.

7. Shape the wire into a circle and join the two ends by twisting together.

8. Curl the twisted wire into a hook/loop shape. Twist again to secure and close the loop. Then cut off any spare pieces of wire that stick out from the end using your pliers.

9. Check that the shape of the wreath is still circular and then string a length of thread through the loop of wire at the top to hang or hang directly using the loop.

Tip:

Try to keep the spacing between your buttons regular and keep them packed tightly together for the best effect. If you want to alternate smaller and larger buttons, why not give it a try!

ORIGAMI STARS

It's beginning to look a lot like Christmas...

Tools and Materials:

- Off-cuts of Christmas wrapping paper
- Craft knife or scissors
- Ruler (metal or a patchwork ruler)
- Needle and thread

This decoration is constructed from 5 separate 'points' that are then joined together at the end to create the final star. Use the photos below as a guide to folding. This is a great design for using up small scraps of paper once you have finished your present wrapping! Place your star on the top of the tree or string up with thread. Let's get folding....

Susan

Instructions

1. Cut out 5 x 3inch squares of wrapping paper. Try to make these squares as accurate as possible to assist with the folding process. The best way to achieve this is to use a ruler and craft knife, rather than scissors.

2. Take the first square of paper and fold in half diagonally, crease and then unfold.

3. Fold in the two edges towards the centre fold you just created. Crease and unfold.

4. Fold over the flap on the right hand side.

5. Tuck that flap under the right hand point and flatten.

6. Fold over the left hand flap over the top.

7. Fold the whole piece in half (left side over to the right).

8. Fold up the bottom edge lining up the fold with the edge of the paper below.

Tip:
You can always use larger pieces of wrapping paper as your starting point. This will make the star larger!

ORIGAMI STARS

9. Fold the little triangle of paper that's sticking out to the left over to the right, lining up your fold with the long straight edge of the triangle that is on the left.

10. Let go of the point of the star and let it unfold slightly so the triangle is more 3D in shape. This point of the star is now complete and we are looking at the back of the point.

11. Create 4 more identical points using the remaining 4 squares of your wrapping paper. Use the instructions from points 2–10 and the photos as a guide.

12–13. We will now start to construct the star. Take two of your origami points and keep them facing away from you (the same way around that we constructed them). On one of the points lift up the flap on the right hand side and slide in the left side of the second point into the space. Use the photos as a guide.

14. Join the third point to the first two. Then keep going until all 5 points are joined together.

15. Join the first and fifth points so that the whole star is constructed.

16. Turn the star over to the right side. Thread your needle with white thread. Make a small hole 5mm near the top of one point of the star with your needle and push the white thread through. Create a loop by knotting together the ends of the string. Trim off the excess thread to neaten.

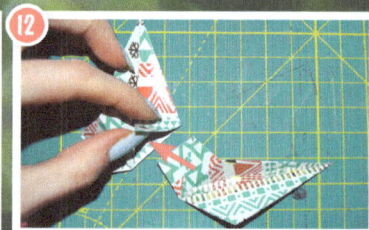

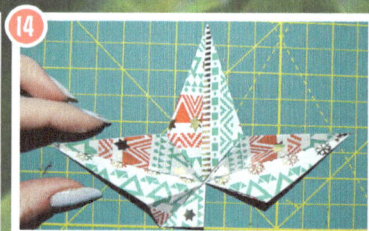

Did You Know?

Manufactured Christmas tree ornaments were first sold by Woolworths in 1880.

Origami Stars (p.96–98)

Templates

Note: Templates are at 100% (no need to scale)

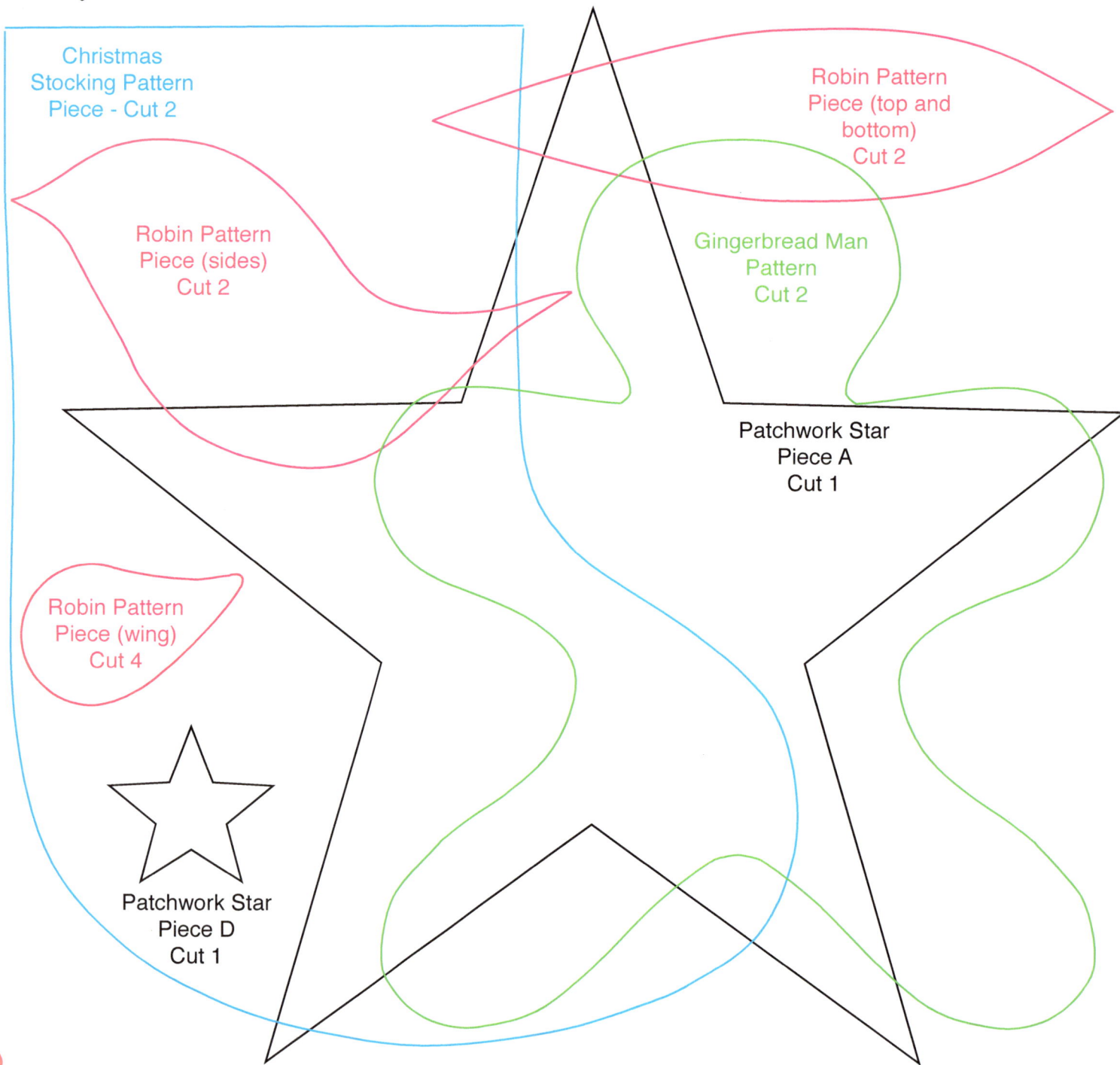

Christmas Stocking Pattern Piece - Cut 2

Robin Pattern Piece (top and bottom) Cut 2

Robin Pattern Piece (sides) Cut 2

Gingerbread Man Pattern Cut 2

Patchwork Star Piece A Cut 1

Robin Pattern Piece (wing) Cut 4

Patchwork Star Piece D Cut 1

Templates

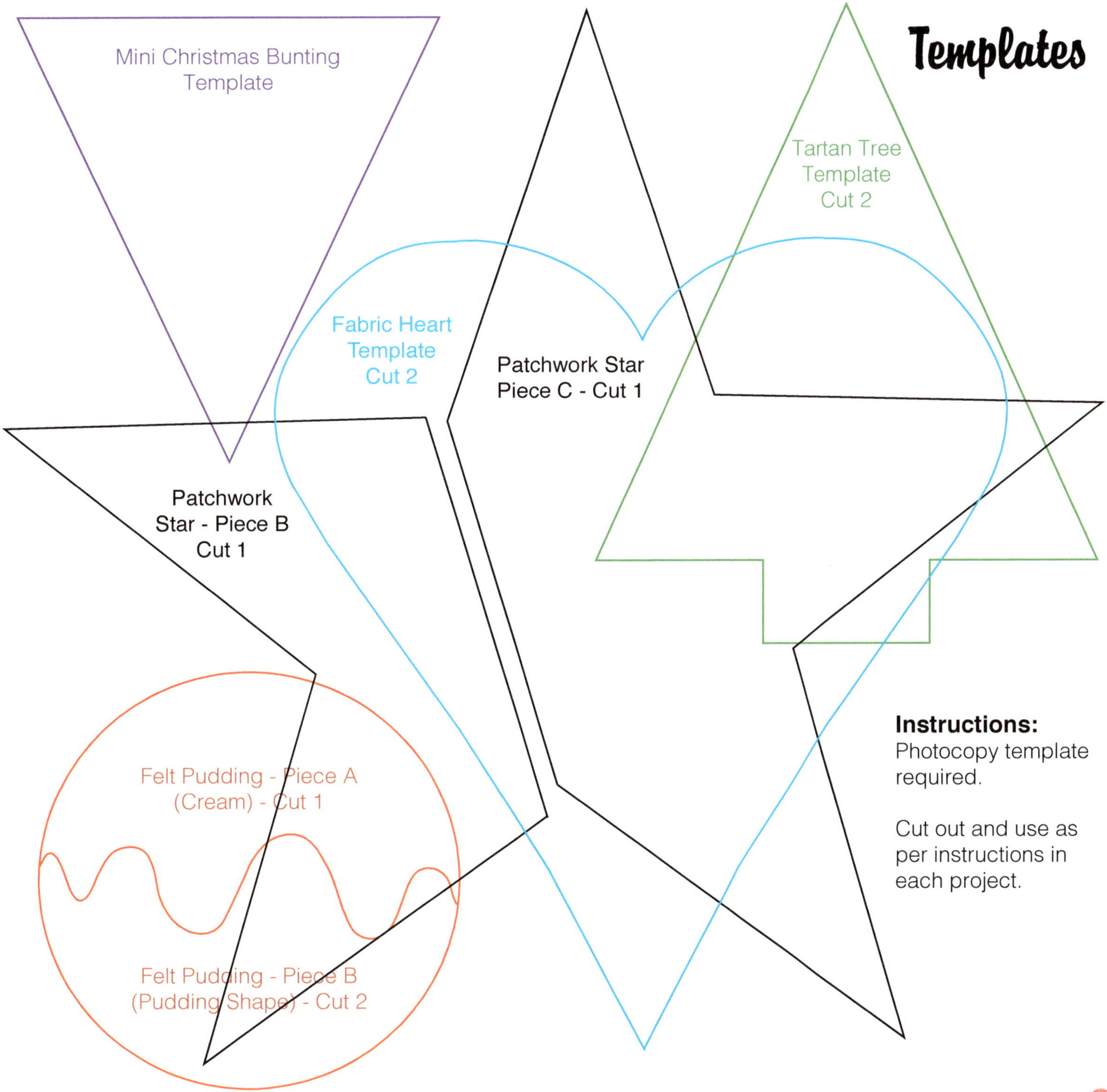

Mini Christmas Bunting
Template

Tartan Tree
Template
Cut 2

Fabric Heart
Template
Cut 2

Patchwork Star
Piece C - Cut 1

Patchwork
Star - Piece B
Cut 1

Felt Pudding - Piece A
(Cream) - Cut 1

Felt Pudding - Piece B
(Pudding Shape) - Cut 2

Instructions:
Photocopy template
required.

Cut out and use as
per instructions in
each project.

How-To Guides

A few handy pointers to help you with some of the projects in this book…

Sewing Guides

Blanket Stitch

Used in the Gingerbread Man (p.30) and Christmas Pudding (p.34) projects.

Tie a knot in the end of your thread. For the first stitch, take the needle from back to front. NB. In the case of our Gingerbread man and Christmas pudding you would only pierce through the first layer of felt so that the knot is enclosed in the middle of the decoration rather than at the back. For the second passing of the needle, move along 5mm and go from front to back, catching the loop of the thread with your needle as it comes back up and before you pull the thread fully through. The first stitch always looks a little funny so don't panic. Repeat the second step again i.e. move along 5mm and pass the needle from front to back catching the loop with your needle as it comes back up and before pulling the thread fully through. This stitch now looks like a full blanket stitch… continue to the end of your work and cast off.

Invisible stitch

To close up a hole in the side of a piece of work e.g. Fabric Hearts (p.28) and Tartan Trees (p.42).

Thread your needle. Tie a knot in the end of your thread. Pass the needle from the wrong side to the right side so that the knot hides inside the decoration you are sewing (i.e. on the wrong side). Using your fingers, hold the two pieces of fabric together where you want them to be. Take the needle and catch a small amount (2-3mm) of one side of the two pieces of fabric passing the needle through the front to the back and back out again in one go. Then catch a small amount of the second side in the same way. Continue along the two edges that you are joining, catching a piece of one side and then the other until the hole closes. When you reach the end, cast off and trim off the excess thread. The stitches should be nearly invisible.

Crochet Explanations (UK Terms)

Please find below simple written instructions on many of the crochet stitches used within the book. Please see **www.magenta-sky.com** for short video tutorials on many of these basic stitches.

ss = slip stitch

Used to join one stitch to another e.g. at the end of a round when working in circles.

Insert hook through the stitch you wish to join to. Yarn over hook and pull through all loops/stitches on the hook.

ch = chain stitch

Most crochet projects start with chain stitch. Used to create a string of stitches or at the start of rows to equate to a full crochet stitch such as a dc or tr. e.g. 3ch = tr.

Start with a slip knot or a stitch of some description on your hook. Yarn over hook. Pull the yarn through the slip-knot or stitch on your hook and you have created a 'chain'. Usually you continue for one or more stitches according to your pattern – yarn over hook and pulling through to create a new chain stitch each time.

dc = double crochet

A standard crochet stitch used in Amigurumi crochet and many other crochet projects.

Put hook through next stitch from front to back. Yarn over hook and pull through hook so that you have 2 loops on the hook. Yarn over hook and pull through those 2 loops.

htr = half treble

A crochet stitch that is height-wise in between the dc and tr stitches.

Yarn over hook, put hook through the next stitch from front to back. Yarn over hook and pull through. There are now 3 loops on the hook. Yarn over hook and pull through all 3 loops.

tr = treble crochet

A standard crochet stitch used a lot in granny square patterns.

Yarn over hook, put hook through the next stitch from front to back. Yarn over hook and pull through. There are now 3 loops on the hook. Yarn over hook and pull through 2 loops only. There are now 2 loops on the hook. Yarn over hook and pull through final 2 loops.

dtr = double treble

A tall crochet stitch.

Yarn over hook twice. Put hook through the next stitch from front to back. Yarn over hook and pull through. There are now 4 loops on the hook. Yarn over hook and pull through 2 loops only. There are now 3 loops on the hook. Yarn over hook and pull through 2 loops only. There are now 2 loops on the hook. Yarn over hook and pull through final 2 loops.

trtr = treble treble

A very tall crochet stitch.

Yarn over hook three times. Put hook through the next stitch from front to back. Yarn over hook and pull through. There are now 5 loops on the hook. Yarn over hook and pull through 2 loops only. There are now 4 loops on the hook. Yarn over hook and pull through 2 loops only. There are now 3 loops on the hook. Yarn over hook and pull through two loops only. There are now 2 loops on the hook. Yarn over hook and pull through final 2 loops.

inc = increase

Used in crochet patterns to increase the number of stitches.

dc twice into the next stitch. In other words, carry out a normal dc, then rather than moving onto the next stitch, do a second dc in that same stitch (i.e. 1dc becomes 2dc)

dec = decrease or dc2tog = double crochet 2 together (same meaning)

Used in crochet patterns to reduce the number of stitches.

Put hook through next stitch, yarn over hook & pull through, put hook through next stitch, yarn over hook & pull through (3 loops on hook). Yarn over hook & pull through all 3 loops. (i.e. 2dc become 1dc).

Merry Christmas!
Susan